VOICE LESSONS

A passage of hope

Sondra R. Galbraith

Copyrite Sondra Richardson Galbraith 2002
Voice Lessons TXu001069845
2nd printing 2015

All Rights reserved. No part of this book may be reproduced or transmitted in any form or by any means, electronic or mechanical, including photocopying and recording, or by any information storage and retrieval system, without permission in writing from the publisher.

ISBN 978-0-578-17085-5

To Richard—

my love, my strength, who walked beside me every step of the way; to all whose voices have inspired, delighted, tutored, comforted and cheered me.

Those who wish to sing always find a song.
-Swedish Proverb

Introduction

It has been sixteen years since I first picked up a notebook and pen to begin *Voice Lessons,* completing it several years later. I had minimal copies printed for family and friends. Recently re-reading my manuscript, I was impressed with the current relevance of the subject matter and feel persuaded the book's message may inform and touch hearts beyond my own circle.

The book relates my journey of raising a child suffering a disability and my dealing with a long-term illness. It contains the insights and lessons these experiences taught me. Mixed within the experiences, I hear the voices of family members and others who colored these experiences with their own perspective and beliefs.

Voice Lessons intertwines these themes. With the prevalence of chronic illness, children who suffer a wide range of disabilities, developing medical advances, and people facing challenge and difficulty in their lives, the book likely touches on something that affects you or someone you know and love.

Contents

	Beginnings	1
1	Who Will You Be?	7
2	Dark Ages	15
3	Light	25
4	Happy Days	33
5	Dark Nights	52
6	Life Goes On	63
7	Summer Days	73
8	Journey Resumes	84
9	Lifestyle	93
10	Farewell	103
11	Send Off	117
12	Pitfalls	128
13	Insights	140
14	Missing Us	150
15	Bus Ride	162
16	Joy and Pain	173
17	Answers	187
18	Yo-Yo's, Deck Chairs and Tulips	200
19	Endings	209
20	Universal Melodies	218
	Catching Up	i
	Acknowledgements	ix
	Addendum	xi
	Endnotes	xxi

I
1969—1977

With the force of a sucker-punch, the doctor's words slammed into my viscera. "Your baby has a birth defect."

My journey of enlightenment began.

Voices Within

BEGINNINGS

When I was a little girl, as soon as summer vacation arrived, my folks loaded our grey 1942 Plymouth and with my three brothers, my sister and me crammed inside, we headed for our Lake Arrowhead cabin high in the mountains above San Bernardino, California.

Winding down the hills of our neighborhood onto Sunset Boulevard, we'd skirt downtown Los Angeles and before long, pass through miles of orange groves and a thousand acres of vineyards.

Beyond San Bernardino we zig-zagged the mountainside. More often than not, Dad pulled off at the halfway point to cool the engine and fill the hissing radiator from the canvas water bag slung across the front grill. We youngsters bounded from the car to stretch our fidgety legs.

Finally, driving through towering pines which almost obscured the sky, windows rolled down to the pristine air, we followed the beautiful lakeshore. Veering off to Cedar Glen, we passed the riding stable, store, and tiny post office and chugged up the steep incline—arriving at last.

Voices Within

Mouse traps emptied and cob webs swept away, we settled in for a glorious summer, sun-drenched and lazy. Dad commuted from his office, joining us on weekends.

The original owner of our log cabin had left treasures in the attic. We'd discovered an ancient wind-up Victrola phonograph with its long Edison-style fluted amplifier and a stack of dusty records. The songs were unfamiliar: *In a Monastery Garden,* for starters. The singers' voices sounded tinny and somewhat distorted. Adding insult, we kids delighted in speeding the turntable with our fingers raising the voices several octaves to a frenzied, madcap rendition, or slowing them to a low, mournful dirge.

Several records were cracked, the resulting click-click-click a distraction and annoyance. Worse were records with a nick or a deep scratch, for the armature would stick, repeating a word over and over.

Minds are like a record player—you've heard the analogy. Each of us creates our own 'records' to play. Early-on, we listened to conversation and internalized feelings and issues of those around us.

The voices of parents, siblings, teachers and peers left deep grooves that influenced our self-perception and helped define our world. They helped establish our self talk, the creation of our *own* voices. It's no surprise that we first learned how to 'talk to ourselves' as a result of how we were talked to.

We may not be consciously mindful of or tuned into the voices etched within our brains. It takes awareness to recognize and pay attention to our voices—and deal with them. No easy task. Some voices, like that pile of old records left in the attic are perhaps distorted, frenzied or mournful. Some, akin to a chipped groove, may drum over and over inside our brain, etching self-fulfilling prophecy. We may listen to songs that diminish rather than nourish and heal our soul. These records should be discarded. Other recordings we would do well to dust off, put in our valued collection, and play often.

I recall the precise moment when the thought occurred to me that in thirty-one years of life I had not yet experienced adversity. I have no idea why the revelation came at that moment, but into my mind popped a sentence I'd once heard. "If you haven't experienced trial or suffering, *you will*." Sure, I'd encountered life's little challenges and disappointments. Who hadn't? However, life presents vigorous soul-stretching and with such work-outs come accompanying aches and pain, likely deep pain. That is how life is set up; one of its grand purposes—through adversity come our greatest lessons and growth. This I knew. But in my generation, conversation about self-awareness and the understanding of how to do actual *soul-work* (recognizing and healing issues of the past) scarcely existed.

In the sixties, there was no such thing as a Self Help Section in the bookstore. I had never meditated, never intentionally taken my mind and body to a place of well-being, peace and stillness. I had never gone 'within.'

During my early years, "*The Law of the Harvest*" and the maxim "*As a man thinketh, so is he,*" had been planted in my mind, but these concepts remained uncultivated. My life flowed smoothly. No circumstance had yet caused examination of my own thought process. No *ahhhh haaaaa's* had lit my brain—that what I expect I get; what I say I create; what I fear, I attract. I alone am responsible for my thoughts and feelings. As surely as I breathe, I reap what I sow. This was the law of the harvest.

Experientially, of course, these and other principles had been in force in my life—they always are, with or without awareness. With a husband I loved and who also adored me, four precious children, a full and busy life, I was happy and content. My journey of enlightenment had not yet begun.

A year and a half later I gave birth to our 5th child, Jonathan, born with Down Syndrome and additional brain damage. Along with the challenges, our little son brought tremendous joy, delight and abundant blessings. He took our hands and walked our family to a place of greater learning, of greater love and gratitude.

Nearly a decade after his birth, weakness, marrow deep, began sucking life from my bones. Month after month I became more debilitated, my illness a mystery. Over a year passed and I remained undiagnosed. I was a very sick girl. *What was wrong with me?*

Finally, it occurred to me to ask a different question. Several questions. Why was I sick? How was I responsible? What was I supposed to be learning? What was really going on? With these questions I took my first steps toward enlightenment.

Things were looking up at the bookstore, too. I acquired my first self help book explaining how to still the mind, achieve full relaxation and become aware of thoughts and feelings submerged deeper than the conscious mind. I could now begin uncovering the layers to find the voices within. I could remove protective layers to discover the real me.

I was well aware of my weaknesses, faults and foibles. What concerned me, now, were the things of which I was not aware. The thought of exposing the whole of my true self, coming face to face, learning who I really was brought great vulnerability. What if I didn't like what I saw? Those voices within, what if I didn't like what I heard? Unsettling business, this. At least there weren't skeletons in my closet—*were there*?

Eventually, I realized that discovering the truth of who I was need not be frightening if, for the journey, I packed a full supply of charity, compassion, forgiveness and mercy. Crossing my fingers and taking a deep breath I plunged in—an Alice in Wonderland falling to the unknown.

I've picked up my pen this August of 1999 to record my journey. I lie in bed, where I have spent a great many of my days for twenty-two years, writing longhand in my *College Ruled 3 Subject Notebook* resting on my legs—drawn up to make a support. I will write as long as my hand and brain can manage. I will write of lessons and the struggle and pain it took to learn them.

Why on earth would I lay-bare experiences so personal? Because I trust the reader will receive my words with respect. Because, when I put into word or thought experiences which have deeply touched me,

Voices Within

I come to a greater understanding of and gratitude for the lessons learned.

My journey, your journey, is the thrill of a lifetime. As we begin to peel back layers to the voices within and discover what has been recorded, we are able to label then sort our records. We choose what to discard. What to play. Soon we create new songs to sing. When we face and heal our past (every human being wrestles with issues—big or small), when we take full responsibility and stewardship for our own life, we are able to joyfully meet and embrace our inner-self. We discover the nobility and magnificence of ourselves, and find the authentic purpose and meaning of our life.

I trust you will find application from the lessons and universal truths explored within these pages; that you will find greater understanding, compassion and patience for those suffering chronic illness; that you will find insight and sensitivity for people suffering disabilities—and for the loved ones to whom they belong.

You will hear the voices of those who have touched my life. You will hear my voice. Listening to songs which nourish the soul, you will hear your own voice.

Who Will You Be?

1

Out the window under shady branches, I could see David sitting beside Millie, our brown and white Sheltie. Millie's head was cocked, ears pricked as she listened to David's jabbering. They were the same age, two now, and although Millie was the beloved family dog her heart belonged to David. Kindred spirits, they were also alike in sweetness and good nature.

Past the forsythia, lilac and primrose bordering the lawn, our acre of land sloped away then spread itself into a paradise of possibility. Here, the pigeon coop stood. There, fox holes and underground huts had been dug. Now, Scott and Mark, nine and eight respectively, worked on a tree house in the gnarly old apple tree. I could hear the hammering. Undoubtedly our only daughter Kristen, our five-year-old tomboy, was alongside, handing up tools or pounding a crooked nail. Still feeling delight in our new home and neighborhood, our family had been settled in for over a year.

Scott was the perfect child—obedient, responsible and respectful.

Who Will You Be?

We *do* that to our firstborn, don't we? And if we and they are lucky, they survive without damage. Surviving—steady, gentle, quiet—Scott was slim, dark in coloring and favoring both parents, had one brown and one blue eye. Early on, he'd become a proficient handy man, tutored at his father's side.

Mark was our only blonde, with large and blue-bright eyes. Creative and possessing a lively curiosity, Mark's artistic gift had been evident from the first crayon up. Like his brother, he was becoming a fine craftsman for one so young.

I stepped outside to check progress on the tree house. Scooping little David into my arms, I twirled him about, patted Millie, stepped to the knoll and shaded my eyes to the sun. The boys were finishing the framework, after initial help from their dad. Kristen raced up the hill. She had begun lessons at the university's Children's Dance Theatre. Tiny, with dark eyes and a shy smile, Kris twirled and leapt through her day to the music within her heart. Feminine, she would nonetheless choose her brother's toys and play their play over a doll any day.

I sat down on the small cement bridge cupping our irrigation ditch, away from the weeds. Kristen alighted and side-by-side—our knees drawn up, arms draped across, and chins resting atop—we watched the builders. Soon, David and Millie joined us. David was a happy little boy, with light brown hair and soft brown eyes. I tousled David's hair, gave a hug then gazed back to Scott and Mark, entwined within the tree branches.

Who Will You Be?

Past the field I could see the foothills of our valley rising to the western slope of the Rocky Mountains. The Wasatch Range rose sharply, towering some 8,000 feet in craggy grandeur. Always the mountain's beauty took away my breath, viewed from this suburb of Salt Lake City, Utah, called Holladay. With the sun warming our faces, Millie contentedly wagging her tail, Kristin, David and I soaked up the glory of summer's end while the boys hammered on. Within days Scott and Mark would be back in school. Why didn't I take more moments like these?

∞∞∞

Several weeks had passed since the older boys had finished the tree house, the September sun sinking a bit further south now as evening approached. It was David's bed time. "Sing, Mommie," David said as we rocked. "Baff song."

"Baff song? Oh," I said, figuring out what he meant. "You want me to sing that silly old song?" David nodded.

> *Alice, where art thou going?*
> *Upstairs to take a bath.*
> *Alice, with legs like toothpicks,*
> *And a neck like a giraffe.*
> *Alice stepped in the bathtub,*
> *Pulled out the stopper plug,*
> *Oh my Goodness, Oh my Soul,*
> *There goes Alice down the hole.*
> *Alice, where art thou going, amen.* [1]

Who Will You Be?

David giggled. I kissed the top of his head. We rocked in silence. "Well, little man," I said, "time to say prayers and hop into bed." A while afterward, Kristen was tucked in with a bedtime story. Two down, two to go. Later, I spent time with the boys, reading Jack London's *The Call of the Wild*.

With the children asleep and the day done, Dick and I lay in bed, he reading the paper, I reading Mitchner's *Hawaii*. I laid my book on the night stand and turned off my lamp. Just the side of Dick's face was visible, his profile in shadow between newspaper pages. I knew every inch of that face. Except for his wearing horned-rimmed glasses, Dick hadn't changed much from one particular afternoon of 1957.

I had just finished two years of college in Utah that June day. This would be my second summer staying with my delightful Aunt Virginia Richardson in Salt Lake, as I'd managed securing jobs both summers. Although I'd miss my parents, if I'd waited to seek employment in Boise, Idaho while living at home, part-time work would undoubtedly have been scarce or nonexistent.

Aunt Virginia had red hair, large, expressive blue eyes and kind arms that had graciously opened themselves to this waif away from home. It was the end of May and my sophomore year. Exhausted, I dropped my suitcases on Aunt Virginia's floor, looking forward to a hot bath and doing absolutely nothing. The phone rang.

"Hi. Is this Sandra?"

Who Will You Be?

"...Yes." (The mispronunciation of Sondra clued-me-in this guy didn't know me.)

"This is Dick Galbraith. You might not remember, but I met you last year at Don and Gretel's wedding reception?"

"Ah..."

"Would you like to go to dinner and a show this coming Friday?"

"I'm sorry. I'm ... going to be busy," I pleasantly replied. (I was.)

"What about Saturday?"

"I'm really sorry. I just walked in from school ... and I've got a bunch of stuff to do—getting settled."

"Next Saturday, then?" the charming voice persisted. "Surely that's enough time."

"Look, I—"

"Oh, come on. What have you got to lose?" the voice interrupted with a chuckle. "I'll pick you up at seven."

"Really, I—"

"I'll see you at seven."

I was furious. The more I thought, the madder I got. Always, I'd had trouble saying no, from salesmen to favor seeker. I yanked up my bags, stumbling toward the bedroom I used. *"Might not remember?" Who was this guy?* I didn't even remember his name. Was it ... Dave? Dave something-or-other. Fumbling for excuses. Feeling an obligation to explain. Why can't I simply say *no*?

Dick hadn't remembered my name, either. Several days before

Who Will You Be?

that fateful phone call, Dick had bumped into his old friends Don and Gretel. They remembered a close-version of my first name, no last name, but approximately where I'd been living. The three of them cruised the steep streets near Aunt Virginia's. "I think that's the house," Don cried after having driven the street twice.

Dick knocked at the next door neighbor who knew I was expected after finals. He acquired all pertinent data, including Aunt Virginia's phone number. *We were engaged in early August and married the end of October.* Dick was an old bachelor, soon to be twenty eight. I would turn twenty a week after our wedding.

While Dick continued reading the paper, with my reverie finished, I reached over and threaded my fingers through the fine blonde hair belonging to the man I loved. Plumping my pillow, I stretched and relaxed into the delicious comfort of our bed.

It had been a quiet day with the boys back in school, while David napped and Kristen played with her Little Kiddles and squat troll doll, its yellow hair shooting straight up like a geyser. Today I'd finished making a doll house out of wooden apple crates—wallpapered and carpeted now, complete with plastic shower curtain in the tiny bathroom. Kristen had been enthralled.

Indeed, it had been too quiet around the house. "Honey, I want another baby." With that announcement the newspaper came down. "What do you think?" I asked.

Dick folded the paper and tossed it aside, then turned to me. All along we'd planned on having five or six children, so my comment

Who Will You Be?

was not shocking, just unexpected. "Well, I guess it's about the right timing, huh?" Dick answered.

"I think so. My arms are getting anxious for a tiny one."

"It's great with me, sweetheart," Richard said. "It's really your decision."

"Okay. Let's put in an order for a little sister for Kris."

Dick turned off his light and snuggled next to me, kissing my cheek. We lay quietly, caught in our own thoughts. Then he whispered, "Just exactly when were you planning on starting this baby?"

∞∞∞

At the first sign of pregnancy, despite the accompanying *yuck*, my heart flooded with gratitude and awe. A literal part of me and Dick was united now in genetic wonder. Hundreds of cells were multiplying daily to form our baby, a unique soul never known to the world, never to be duplicated. There is a singular bonding only a mother can know. From the first recognizable flutter of tiny arm or leg, on to hiccoughs and feats of gymnastic prowess, my babies' hearts and mine beat in rhythmic harmony.

Dick and I made our share of mistakes as we practiced parenthood on our innocent, vulnerable, dependent little children. We did give each child the gift all children deserve—being wanted and cherished. Despite mistakes we would make in the future—despite

Who Will You Be?

the hazards, the complexities, the momentous demands of parenthood—we looked forward with joy and anticipation to our next child.

∞∞∞

Five times I had fixed a nursery. Paint on the rocker, crib and dresser had dried and I'd lugged each inside, then hung pictures and curtains. Next, I'd tenderly placed the baby clothes, old and new, into the drawers. At last, my bulging pounds anchoring me to the rocking chair, taking a deep breath I surveyed my work. Good. Now, all I had to do was wait.

Who *are* you, my precious? I can hardly wait to hold you. Kiss the soft nape of your neck. Count your toes. Nurse you. Sing you a lullaby. Love you.

Dark Ages

2

JANUARY, 1970. Waiting ended too soon. Morning arrived and with it, imminent birth. For the first time, Richard was in the delivery room, husbands just recently allowed. "Are you okay, honey?" It was my question. Bound in green gown and cap, Dick's face looked much the same hue.

I was five weeks early. Even so, the baby was unusually small. Dr. Phillip Clark, personal friend and Ob-Gyn, had ordered emergency respiratory equipment and alerted standby personnel.

I began to hemorrhage. "We've got placental abruption," Phil said to his nurse, who clapped an oxygen mask on my face. "Okay, Sondra. Bear down again." The baby's head came. "*Damn*, there's a cord here." Phil cried. "Try to hold off. I've got to loosen it, *now*."

Dick gripped my hand. "The cord's wrapped around twice," Dr. Clark explained, while his gifted, swift fingers worked. "Come on. Come on," he mumbled as he pulled slack from the cord—fed—loosened, pulled—fed—loosened. "There! Okay, Sonie, all the way now."

It had been nearly impossible to keep from bearing down. *Yeah, right*, I'd thought. In an instant, the thought was crowded out by anxiety. I darted a glance at my husband, chalk-white now. My heart was in my throat. All night I'd prayed for our baby. Please be all right, little sweetheart.

One last bearing down and my job was done. "Ah. You have a son." Phil smiled. "If you hadn't come early," he said, cutting the umbilical, "the baby would likely have strangled. Nature knows what it's doing."

Finally, with the mask removed, I could ask, "*Is he okay?*"

"I think he'll be fine. He's sure active."

I threw Dick a grin. "Fine time you pick coming to delivery. All the commotion." I pulled his hand close, kissing it. "Another boy," I said, relief spilling tears.

Dr. Clark placed our baby in my arms. He was beautiful. My son's eyes opened wide for a moment, and locked onto mine. From my very being, I felt he saw me. "Just a second, now," Dr. Clark said. "We need him on oxygen." Then he was whisked away.

∞∞∞

In recovery, a nurse checked my vital signs, stepped aside and turned back as the intercom crackled a message: "Move Mrs. Galbraith to room 507." Hefted onto a narrow gurney, I was wheeled through busy corridors and parked into a small, windowless room, fluorescent light buzzing.

Dark Ages

What was wrong? Anxious minutes dragged until Dr. Clark and Richard walked in. Richard took my hand, his face ashen.

I need to tell you something about the baby," Phil began. *My son had died.* "Sondra, your baby is a mongoloid."

A mongoloid? A baby that develops an enlarged head? "... I'm not exactly sure what a mongoloid is," I said.

"A mongoloid is mentally retarded, usually with physical problems as well." Phil swallowed hard then plunged ahead. "One trait is their rather slanted eyes and short stature, resembling a person of the Mongolian race."

Of course. I knew that. For a second I was mixed up with . . . hydrocephalic. I even remembered that word. Part of my mind continued walking away in this direction. I had to pull myself back; even so, Phil's voice seemed to come from afar—the impact of his words barely registering. "Is . . . he going to be all right? I mean, being premature . . . and the cord and everything?" Tears welled.

"He's a strong little guy. His lungs and heart are doing fairly well, all things considered."

"Did the cord cause oxygen deprivation?"

"Probably." Phil knew the gist of my question. "But if there's brain damage it will likely be hard to assess." Visibly shaken, Dr. Clark gave my shoulder a squeeze. "Damn. I'm so sorry."

I nodded, brushing away the tears. "What causes it?"

"We don't know, really. Soon after conception the 21st chromosome fragments somehow and every cell ends up with an

Dark Ages

extra chromosome."

Dick sat on the bedside now, still grasping my hand. Dr. Clark clapped Dick's shoulder, took a deep breath and said, "Well, you two need to be alone. I'll check back tonight."

He was nearly outside. "Phil." He turned back. "Thanks. We could have lost him if you weren't so terrific," I said. Dr. Clark nodded then closed the door. My husband enfolded me into the comfort of his arms and together we wept.

Lying back on the bed I took Dick's hands into mine. Careful of stitches and after-pains, I gingerly shifted myself. "Here, lie beside me. You're exhausted." Settled now, I draped my arm across Dick's chest and kissed him on the cheek.

Dick's mother, a widow, lived in Salt Lake. My parents had recently moved to Utah. We were grateful to have them near. "Have you called the folks yet?" I asked.

"No."

"After you call them, what about calling the office and a couple of friends and have them spread the word?" Dick nodded. "Tell them we're doing good and not to feel awkward about it or anything."

We lay side-by-side, quiet for a moment. "I'm so sorry, sweetheart," Dick said.

"Me too. I . . . I wonder if I did something wrong? Took some drug, or something. I had a shot for that strep infection, before I knew I was pregnant."

"No, you didn't do anything."

Dark Ages

I took a deep breath, letting it slowly ebb. Dick was right. It was no one's fault. We'd not play a guilt game. We would focus on our baby. Dick led us in prayer for our little son's well being.

Sooner or later some circumstance smacks us into realignment—purifying the focus of mind and heart, illuminating truest, innermost feelings. The love and gratitude I had for my husband drew forth the most tender emotions of my heart. Together, we could handle anything. Together we were whole.

Dick took my hand, kissed it and placed it on the side of his cheek. "Guess I'd better make those calls. Are you all right?"

"Sure. It's going to be okay, honey."

A hundred thoughts were racing in my mind when Dick returned. "Did you reach my mom?" Dick nodded. "What did she say?"

"Oh, sweetheart, of course she felt terrible. She really couldn't say much but she took it well. You know your mom. My mother was really shook . . . " Dick stopped to gain composure, then recounted the other calls.

We'd had two names in mind. Neither of them seemed right now, so we browsed the baby pamphlet. There it was: *Jonathan, gift from God.* Again we held each other for a time. "You look terrible, honey," I said finally. "Go home, take a nap. Be there when the kids get home from school." I could feel Dick's hesitation. "Go. I'm fine. Come back when things are settled." A stab ripped my heart, bringing fresh tears. "Give the kids a hug. Tell them I love them and miss them." Wiping my eyes dry I said, "You know, Jonathan's going to be a

Dark Ages

great blessing in all our lives."

∞∞∞

My emotions see-sawed throughout the day. Blessings notwithstanding it was rotten, lousy luck. I lay grieving for the life my baby would never have. I'm so sorry, Jonathan.

"Mrs. Galbraith?" Opening my eyes I saw my pediatrician looming beside me. I was in the maternity ward now. Condolences were offered and the latest news on Jon's condition. He said, "You'll want to place your baby in the State Training School of course."

"*What?*"

"You're not planning on taking your baby home?" His words were intended as a statement rather than a question. "It would probably be easiest if you didn't see him." He spoke softly, gently. Nonetheless, my mouth gaped open.

Mustering as much kindness as possible, I replied, "Of course we're taking him home. He's our son."

"Mrs. Galbraith, this is a matter deserving great consideration. You have no idea what you might be getting yourself into….and your family."

"Well, there's really no consideration. I'd like to see my boy as soon as possible. When might that be?"

"In a few days, when he's stabilized."

"I'm planning on breast feeding. That won't be a problem will it?"

"Actually, it will. He's mongoloid and premature. His sucking reflex will be particularly weak. And he'll be in the hospital for days. Once babies start the bottle they usually won't nurse," he explained. "It just isn't practical. I'm sorry."

"Well, I'd like to try. I could use a breast pump and come to the hospital once a day. Couldn't that work?"

"It's doubtful, but you could try, I suppose." Ready to leave now, the doctor again advised, "Mrs. Galbraith, down the road it might truly be necessary to place your son. No one knows future circumstances. You've got a husband and other children to consider. Just remember that, all right?"

Years later I would remember his prophetic words. For now, they smacked of defeatism. Whatever happened to hope? To hard work? Sacrifice? Accountability? My heart swelled fiercely. *You're going to be fine, Jonathan. Mama won't let anything happen to you. I'll always take care of you. I love you, Jonathan J.*

∞∞∞

For just an instant, at the very beginning, I had wondered—can I love you, baby? Can I handle this? The thought dissolved as lightning-fast as it had come. *I love my baby.* From the moment I knew I was expecting I had loved my baby.

We would all handle it. By now, Kristen and David knew. I

Dark Ages

looked at my watch. Soon the boys would be home from school, Dick taking them in his arms and telling them about their sweet little brother. Already, support from loved ones was easing the way. Bouquet after gorgeous bouquet had arrived and I'd received a number of phone calls.

Naturally every caller was apprehensive. What courage and love it had taken for each to pick up the phone and dial. How many times had I not reached out to others because I didn't know what to say? Because I didn't want to chance sticking my foot in my mouth? No more. In a lifetime, we all say and hear trite, patronizing, ill-chosen words; as speaker needs courage, listener needs charity—together each focusing on the sweet intent of the heart.

Voice lessons had begun. Deep within me flooded the realization that I could never judge others in similar circumstances. What was right for me and my family might not be so for others. My upbringing, personality and perception were singular to me. I also knew there would be no question in Dick's mind whether or not to bring Jonathan home. Never would I assume all should think and feel as we. No, there would be nothing but compassion for others facing institutionalization of a child. I understood, too, that my doctor had sincerely advised what he perceived best. I wept for us all.

Dark Ages

It seems unbelievable the word *mongoloid* had not instantly registered with me. I was not the exception, however. Society was barely emerging from the Dark Ages in its knowledge, perception and treatment of the mentally and physically disabled. There was limited interface with handicapped persons. I'd had none.

Devouring leaflets my pediatrician left, I was relieved to encounter the term, 'Down Syndrome'—named for the physician who first researched the congenital disorder. I abhorred *mongoloid.* To me the word was an affront to both race and individual. Still, an arduous struggle lay ahead: mankind's step to embrace the preciousness and dignity of every single child of God on the earth.

∞∞∞

Through the window I watched as dusk slowly siphoned blue from the sky, leaving winter-grey; far below, city lights pinpointed in the ever-deepening night. It was a long wait until visiting hours, husbands and parents only. What a day.

I brushed back straggly locks of hair and smoothed the rumpled gown, longing for a shower and shampoo. Longing to hold Jonathan. Dr. Clark stepped in, noting the mass of flowers. "Hell, looks like somebody died." I laughed. "How are you doing?" he asked.

"Doin' good. Have you checked on my baby?"

"He's developing jaundice, but he's under the lights now. That should take care of it." Otherwise, Jonathan was continuing to

Dark Ages

stabilize, his prognosis encouraging. After a brief chat, Phil left, and to my joy, Dick appeared.

"I snuck in," he said, pulling the privacy curtain.

First, I needed the children's reaction—in detail. It had been a tender time of acceptance and tears. My mom was at our home now watching the children and had sent her heartfelt love.

Hours had passed since I'd cried. Glancing up, I saw my father. He walked to the bedside, sat, then hugged me. My heart broke, anew. Never had I felt deeper love for him. My father's love and compassion pulsed to my core, and with it came insight. I was still and would always remain his little girl. I glimpsed more clearly the unbroken chain linking parent to child, generation upon generation.

Light

3

When Jon was three days old, after peeking many times through the nursery window, I finally got to hold him. In a private room off the preemie nursery, I scrubbed, donned cap and gown and waited. I thought of our son, Mark, also premature; Dick and I had anxiously watched him through that same window. Minutes dragged. Still I waited for Jonathan.

At last I hold my baby close and feel his warmth. I touch his soft, fine hair. My lips fit sideways on the bridge of his nose, between his faint little eyebrows and I kiss him there, then place his silken cheek next to mine. We rock and I sing a lullaby my father sang:

> *Hush a bye, baby, don't say a word,*
> *Mama's goin' to buy you a mocking bird,*
> *If that mockin' bird don't sing,*
> *Mama's goin' to buy you a diamond ring . . .*[2]

My heart beats against his. He wiggles and I smile. "I love you, Jonathan J.," I say. Again, tears blur my eyes. "What will your life be,

Light

my precious little son?"

∞∞∞

On our way home from the hospital, Jon left behind, Dick and I drove up Olympus Drive to the tall spruce tree that divided the street, circled to the right onto Karren and pulled into our driveway. Dick would unload my over-night case and flowers after helping me inside.

I was seldom away from my children, but seeing them, I experienced a familiar phenomenon: For several moments each looked different. Perhaps I saw them as others did. Always, each child looked bigger, more mature. After hugs and kisses, I embraced my mother, emotions choking my throat. I was so grateful to have my parents living in Salt Lake now, to feel of their tremendous love and support first-hand. We sat and I told them news of Jonathan.

"Mama, isn't our baby glad to be borned? It musta' been dark and squishy in your tummy," David said.

Laughing, Mark jumped in on top of David's comment, "Who does he look like, Mom?"

"Everybody but you," Kristen said. "Mom already told us over the phone. He's got long, dark hair and you were bald."

"Yeah, yeah, I know."

"Well, you had a wispy little blonde fringe," I said, roughing up Mark's hair.

"How retarded will Jonathan be?" was Scott's question, his eyes filled with concern.

Light

"We don't know yet, Scottie. But, we'll hope and pray he'll live quite a normal life," I said.

"Will people make fun of him?"

"Some. They are the ones to feel sorry for, because they lack understanding and compassion. Most will accept Jonny with lots of love."

Later, we sat at the dinner table, ready for a lovely meal neighbors had prepared. The phone rang. "Mrs. Galbraith, this is the hospital. Jonathan's bilirubin count is alarmingly high, and the doctor feels he needs to do a complete blood exchange. I'm sorry, but you'll have to come back so we can do a work-up on you, to check your RH negative factor. You'll need to sign a consent form."

These were anxious hours, but Jonny handled the transfusion well, and my daily visits to nurse him continued the sweet time of bonding. Jon remained in the hospital for almost a month.

∞∞∞

Today's the day. David and Kristen pull the kitchen chairs to the large window, in full view of the driveway.

"Oh, it will be a long time yet," grandma says.

"But we don't want to miss them."

"I'll tell you in plenty of time," grandma assures.

"But, Grandma, what if we don't see them coming?" Kristen asks.

"My baby brother wants to meet me," David adds, sitting himself

Light

down.

They wait, sweet faces beside the window pane. Millie sits close by, on her spot by the side door. David swings his legs. Back and forth. Back and forth. Kris winds a long strand of hair around her finger. Millie rests her head on her paws, ears pricked up and eyes alert. David sighs. Kristen scrapes her chair closer, the window fogging from her breath. She draws a picture upon it, then wipes it clear to see. Longer and longer they wait, an eternity for ones so young.

"Here they come. *Here they come.*" Kristen squeals at last and off the chairs they fly.

MITCHELTORENA ELEMENTARY, Los Angeles, CA. 1942

Mother and I walk through the door where I'll begin my formal education. My eyes take in the large sunlit room with its shelves of books, puzzles and toys; its tables and chairs just my size. Seated with my new classmates, our teacher opens a story book and mother slips away. I am left to get through first-day jitters, a kindergartner at last.

I love the huge wooden blocks. In an instant, I can stack them higher than myself. I love the pungent smell of our individual grass mats placed on the floor at nap time. I love chocolate milk. Of greatest fascination is the kaleidoscope. Taking the long, smooth cardboard tube, I lift it to my

Light

EYE. A DAZZLING PATTERN SPLASHES BEFORE ME. TURNING THE END CAP, AS I'VE SEEN OTHERS DO, THE BITS OF GLASS MESH TOGETHER IN A CONFUSION OF COLOR, THEN SLOWLY THE NEXT PATTERN FORMS—CLEAR AND PRECISE.

*

Life can seem rather like the disarray of fragments before design takes form. Months, years, a lifetime passes for God's grand design to work its magnificence. In the meantime, it was my challenge to figure out and to do my part—make sense of experience—learn, grow and bring clarity of purpose to my life. I would learn that sometimes, all I could do was trust the journey and wait. Voice Lessons. I can choose to listen to the songs in my heart. In the end, all things can work for the good.

∞∞∞

I chop the last of the carrots, dumping them into the soup stock. Jonny lays in his infant carrier atop the counter. I step close. "How ya doin', pumpkin?" I ask, touching his cheek. Jonathan looks at me with nearly a smile, four months old now.

While savoring an unhurried moment, I notice his gaze on me change. As if a veil were opening within his eyes, I see into his soul. His spirit flames through in all its magnificence and nobility—his intelligence unmasking itself in brilliant perfection. "*This is who I am, Mother*," it says.

Light

∞∞∞

In the springtime, after Jon's January birth, I slipped outside for a walk. A movement of air stirred through the great maple trees lining our street, the overhead sun casting a shadow-dance upon the road.

Several days earlier, I had begun to feel an increasing sense of well-being and peace. We all experience periods when life seems particularly harmonious and joyful, when things go well and we might not put our finger on the why of it.

As I felt the sun on my face and looked about my familiar surroundings—like an ordinary day, the joyous feelings in my heart multiplied a thousand fold. I seemed to see by power of the Spirit. Every sense intensified. As all matter emanates its own particular energy frequency, molecules and atoms awhirl, I could *feel* substance. I could *feel* color. The trees were living things. The grasses. The rocks. Experientially, I realized inanimate objects were living things. Not just God's creatures but all of God's creations possessed a spirit-counterpart. Like the psalmist, I could feel of the praise and worship all creation rendered God their Creator.

By my thoughts I communicated with the trees, the grasses, the flowers, expressing delight in them and gratitude for their existence. Likewise, I sensed their delight in my existence. My neighbors' dog, stretched on the lawn, sat up and pricked his ears. *You're a fine fellow and I love you,* my heart sang, and he sent back to me a message of love.

Light

I was astonished. All seemed surreal. At the same time, however, the experience felt normal—seeing, feeling, communicating in this non-verbal manner was second nature. In pre-mortal existence, was this simply a typical way of communication? Of seeing?

A woman and child approached. Strangers, yet into my being flooded recognition. They were my sisters, and I felt infinite love for them. I felt sorrow and compassion for the burdens they carried or would carry; joy for who they were and would become. Each was dear and precious to me.

I wanted to stop the mother and child. To throw my arms around each and say, "Do you have any idea how much God loves you?" I quickly brushed away tears and as they passed I managed to croak a hello.

Only after my walk would I understand the reason for my feelings. Like an emerging pattern in the old kindergarten kaleidoscope, there would be a process of focus before wondrous clarity. In the privacy of my bedroom, I pondered the extraordinary experience. I wept. Just days earlier I'd had the privilege of looking into Jonathan's soul. This day's revelation had something to do with *him*. Everything to do with him. Of course. Instinctively, I'd known it from the beginning. Somehow, the gift of my little son's birth had opened my eyes to see by the Spirit; to catch a glimpse of the pure love of God.

I now had a priceless experience to add to my treasured collection. I uttered a prayer of thanksgiving. Still in awe, I looked

Light

outside my window to the sky, the trees, the tulips. *I pick a tulip blossom and press it in the pages of my heart—to keep in remembrance, forever.*

ooooo

As gradually as my feelings had built, to climax in those profound minutes, they gradually diminished. Time would pass before I fully understood and appreciated the gift I'd received that day.

Through the years I've tried to recapture that quality of pure love, to exercise and feel unconditional charity. I've never come within a fraction. My soul longs to experience once again what I felt. After I breathe my last mortal breath and return *home*, I will experience the full glory of God's love; the full glory of all His creations.

Happy Days

4

1972. Jonathan sat inside a cardboard box, hands cupped over each side, Mark poised at the end. Millie was stretched out by the patio door, slowly wagging her tail back and forth, head cocked at the scene. Making the noise of a revving motor, Mark pushed off, whizzing Jon throughout the house, one end to the other. Jonny's hair flew behind, his face split with a wide grin. Finally, Mark slowed, circled the living room and pulled to a stop. Panting, he dropped spread-eagle on the floor as Jonny rocked back and forth, wanting more. "Race car's outa gas, Jon." It was bath time anyway.

I lifted Jonathan into the tub. He kicked his legs and smacked the water with his hands, laughing as it splashed into our faces. I lathered soap onto a cloth and scrubbed his back, then his thin little arms and legs. Jon was two now and atypically for a Down Syndrome, was very slender and rather tall. Next, I worked on his ears as he squirmed, hollering disapproval. "Rub a dub dub, three men in a tub," I chanted.

Finished, I rinsed Jonathan—skin slick and shiny—and pulled

Happy Days

him, dripping, from the tub. Wrapped in a towel, I hoisted him on top of the toilet lid, the same place my mother used to stand me to wipe me dry. "What a big, fine boy you are," I said. "Mama loves you." I kissed the top of his head, his hair damp and sweet-smelling. Jon looked up and smiled.

Mark was still in the living room, joined by Kris and David. I dropped Jon off with them on my way to fetch his clothes. Loud screams erupted and I rushed back to see what disaster was unfolding. Kristen and David were leaping wildly up and down. Mark was clapping his hands and whistling. Scott had stepped in from another room. Seeing me, each shouted the explanation. *Jon had taken his first wobbly steps at two years of age.* He stood naked in the middle of the frenzy, thinking he'd done something terribly wrong. Dropping down, he began to cry.

Jonathan was a sweet child. He had brown hair, dark eyes, and a beautiful little face and smile. Despite his slender frame, he was unusually strong. Soon after his first steps, Jonny discovered the honey can in the Lazy Susan. Somehow he got the lid off and by the handful slurped its deliciousness—honey dripping off his elbows, honey coating his eyelashes and honey matting his hair. Chuckling, I started to gather him up to head for the tub. Quick as lightening he clamped a hand back on the heavy can, dragging it along the kitchen floor. I sat down, prying his hand off, only to have him grab hold with the other, his fingers tight as a vice. Right hand. Left hand. Right, left—a grown woman unable to peel her little son free.

Happy Days

Millie knew the strength of Jonny's fingers, too. After her first encounter with hair pulling, she kept her distance but loved him nonetheless.

Each of us found delight in Jon's accomplishments, evolving in slow-motion—bringing gratitude and magnified awareness for the wonder and complexity of human development. Jon taught us to plumb deeply within, to draw forth greater patience, understanding and quality of love, a depth unsounded apart from him. He opened wide our vista to view all people with increased empathy and appreciation.

∞∞∞

Wanting to help Jon achieve his potential, I learned of Dr. Henry Turkel in Detroit, Michigan, who specialized in treating Down children with an innovative nutritional, drug-therapy program. The all natural medication was to assist assimilation and help rid the body of harmful metabolites produced by each cell's extra chromosome. After great consideration, Dick and I decided to take Jon to Dr. Turkel. Favorably impressed, we began the therapy before Jon's second birthday. Every four months Jon and I returned to Detroit for testing and evaluation from the kindly old physician. Dr. Turkel, a friend of Linus Pauling (Nobel Peace prize—1962) and Jonas Salk (developer of the polio vaccine), was famous in his own right for inventing a biopsy punch to obtain bone tissue.

Happy Days

Shortly after beginning Jon on Turkel's program, I started Jonathan on a regimen developed by Drs. Doman and Delacado of the *Institute for the Achievement of Human Potential* based in Philadelphia. The program was targeted to improve a variety of brain/neurological impairments: stroke, brain trauma, birth defects, etc.

An infant's brain is not fully developed at birth. Crawling (prone) and creeping (on hands and knees) help complete development. Theoretically, the Institute proposed that by simulating crawling movements, called patterning, damaged brain cells would be stimulated and healthy cells trained to adopt new function.

With help from a dear neighbor, Virginia Warner, we implemented the program. Seventy-two volunteers came weekly to 'pattern' Jon in five-minute sessions, three times daily. As a family, we patterned most Saturdays, nothing on Sundays. Each session required four people—one to manipulate Jon's head, one his feet and a person for each arm. One team member remained at the end of each session to supervise creeping, sensory and hand-eye coordination exercises and so forth.

Soon, our teams were trained and all ran smoothly. Jon built up endurance and calluses on his little knees. It was hard work, but for the most part he was cooperative, extremely patient and good-natured.

How did I manage with people traipsing through the house all day? I became more organized and efficient and planned errands between sessions. The routine became a way of life. It seemed in no way to hamper our lives. It was a privilege to have these wonderful people—teens to elderly—come into our home, serving and caring. Jon enriched their lives, also, as they grew to love him.

In a neighboring city, the Philadelphia Institute had personnel who periodically evaluated Jonny and adjusted Jon's program accordingly. We patterned for nearly two years, with rarely a cancellation. On an occasional no-show, I would fill in. Many of the teams stayed with us the entire time.

Helen Heaton, a close friend, was a team 'lead'. Each week after Jon's session on the Patterning Table where he'd had his therapy, Helen read him *Three Little Kittens*, taking his finger and tapping it on the cover illustration. "Kitty. Kitty," she would say. One day Jon replied, "Kitty, Kitty." The first words he spoke.

Each morning as I entered Jonny's bedroom I said, "H-i-i-i-i-i-i, Jonny." Shortly after uttering his first precious words, he began answering back my morning greeting with a "hi." Next came "Daddy," "Shoe," "Car." Several months later, as unexpectedly as he had begun, he stopped talking, never again to speak a word. In my dreams, on treasured occasions, Jonny talks to me.

∞∞∞

Happy Days

LIBERTY, UTAH, 1973. Another summer had arrived. I was lazily stretched upon a chaise lounge on the back patio of our cabin, engaging in the luxury of total relaxation. The air had cooled, pleasant now. Jonny, who was three years old, played in his small wading pool beside me. He'd splashed out nearly all the water. I'd refill it, eventually. For now, I closed my eyes and sighed a breath of deep contentment.

Magpies quarreled in the nearby cottonwoods. Millie barked somewhere in the distance, ecstatic to be roaming about. Topaz, our horse, switched his tail against a fly as he cropped the pasture grass on the other side of the fence.

We were spending two weeks' vacation at our *cabin*—a misnomer for our second home just an hour's drive away, in the little town of Liberty. It lay high in small, rural Ogden Valley. Cabins sprinkled the mountainsides and the area had two golf courses, winter skiing and a large reservoir used for boating. However, the little farming communities fostered a small-town folksiness that offset any air of resort-town ambience.

We had fifteen acres on the valley floor with a lovely stream that flowed year round. A neighbor used part of our land to raise alfalfa in exchange for keeping an eye on our horses and feeding them through winter.

Early this morning we'd slipped to Pineview Dam for some water skiing. Before long, Scott and Mark would be outshining Dick and me on the slalom. Kris was becoming proficient on two skis and

Happy Days

David was trying to muster the courage for a first attempt. Jonny enjoyed boating but especially loved playing at the water's edge, his only vexation being the bulky orange life-vest that chaffed his chin and hampered his freedom. Finally, I had come to see the beauty of the dam, its barrenness such a contrast to the pine-filled exquisite beauty of the Lake Arrowhead, California, of my youth.

I heard Jonny climb from the pool then patter across the patio. Opening my eyes, I watched him walk towards the horse, stick his arm through the rail fence and reach out to him. Good natured and gentle, Topaz obliged, stepping closer as he continued grazing. He was an old veteran, an Appaloosa once belonging to a sheepherder. He was huge, seventeen hands high. Topaz had a sixth sense about Jonny, ever careful and patient in his presence. He allowed Jonny to pet him—rather a pinch-pull, far from pleasant. Nickering softly, Topaz stepped to the fence within reach. My heart flooded with love for the grand old fellow.

Besides Topaz, we owned Mac, a feisty POA pony, fast as a flash whose shenanigans made us laugh. Cinnamon was our quarter horse bay, steady and dependable. She had given birth to a little filly we named Nutmeg, who had a white diamond on her forehead, just like her mama.

Kristen stood a ways off in the field holding Nutmeg's halter, crooning softly as she used the curry comb. Little Meg shook her head and skittered about on ungainly, stilt-like legs, her tiny, pointed hoofs kicking up puffs of dust. Getting used to the feel of the comb,

Happy Days

Meg settled down, tolerating the grooming.

The sun lowered in the sky, casting a backlight on Kristen's hair, turning it from brown to gold. Down by the brook, I could see the tip of my mother's sun hat. An artist, she sat at her easel working on an oil painting. The folks were up for the week; Mom to paint and Dad to help build our barn along with Dick, Scott and Mark. My father would turn seventy-eight in the fall, yet here he was, lifting heavy beams, sawing and pounding nails. I was amazed and ever so proud of them—an old man, a twelve and thirteen-year-old and my husband building a barn from scratch, with just a blueprint and pile of lumber.

David, Millie by his side, was playing at the stream. Occasionally I caught glimpses of them through clumps of willow. Beyond our property lay an expanse of pasture land, dotted with cows and horses, gently sloping to the river bottom. Venerable cottonwood and elm trees staked the river's meandering course.

Infinite shades of green were spread across the landscape. Along our fence lines where wild daisies grew, a few valiant blooms remained. A small patch of cumulus clouds plumped themselves on the mesa in an otherwise clear and gorgeous sky. My eyes and soul filled with the nourishing serenity and beauty before me. How grateful I was for our valley home, where we could work, play and relax together.

We had over half a year of patterning under our belts and Jonny had returned twice to Dr. Turkel in Detroit. He seemed to be doing fairly well. I had registered Jon in a preschool, Developmental

Happy Days

Disabilities, and at age four he would be admitted, able to have interaction with peers. Our lives were filled with great blessings. All was well.

Finishing his visit with Topaz, Jonny came back and crawled onto my lap. From the barn, another volley of hammering began, bouncing a ringing echo off the house. So much for relaxation. Nearly time to eat, anyway. "Let's go fix dinner, Jon," I said.

Dick's father had passed away when Dick was eighteen. His mother, Eva, remarried a decade later only to have her second husband die within several years. She was a widow again. Jonathan loved his grandmothers, but was especially drawn to my father. Dinner over, Jon was sprawled on Dad's lap, chest to chest, rubbing several little fingers back and forth across Dad's mustache.

"Want Grandpa to sing you a song?" Dad inquired. Of course.

Bill Grogan's goat was feeling fine.
Ate three red shirts right off the line.
Bill took a stick, gave him a whack,
And tied him to the railroad track.

The whistle blew. The train drew nigh.
Bill Grogan's goat was doomed to die.
He gave three groans of awful pain,
Coughed up the shirts, and flagged the train. [3]

"Another one?" Dad asked.

Where was Moses when the lights went out?
Where was he and what was he about? [4]

Happy Days

Voice Lessons. It was as if I'd pulled a cherished record from my collection and put it on to play. As if, years melting away, I was sitting on Dad's lap, listening to his songs, feeling the warmth of his love.

Bedtime. Keeping another family tradition, Jonny faced me then stepped atop my feet, his arms cinched around my legs. I sang, "Walking to bed on Mama's feet, tra la la la la," as we stumbled to the staircase. I zipped up Jon's bunting and lifted him into the crib. "Night, Sweetie," I said. "Mama loves you."

1970 Sondra with Jon

With David and Kristen

Scott, Mark holding Jon, Kristen, David

Mark holding Jon, Dick, Scott, Kristen, David, Sondra

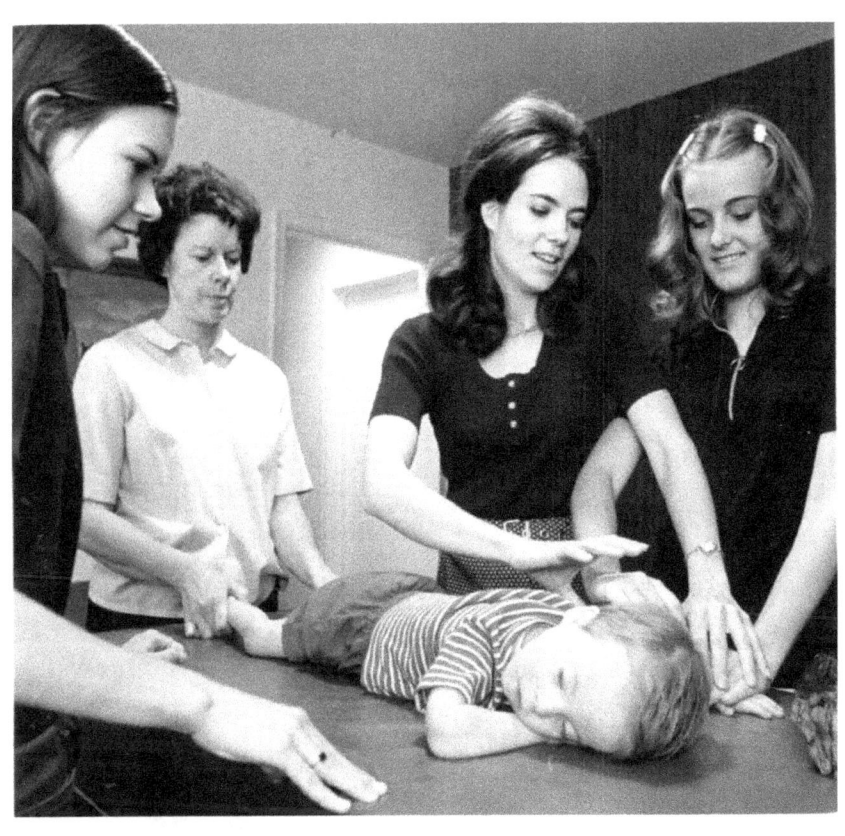

1973 Sondra instructing patterners: (l-r): Wendy Elwood, Jackie Elwood, Sondra, Sherry Fotheringham

Mark and Scott ready for push off; Lovin' reflections

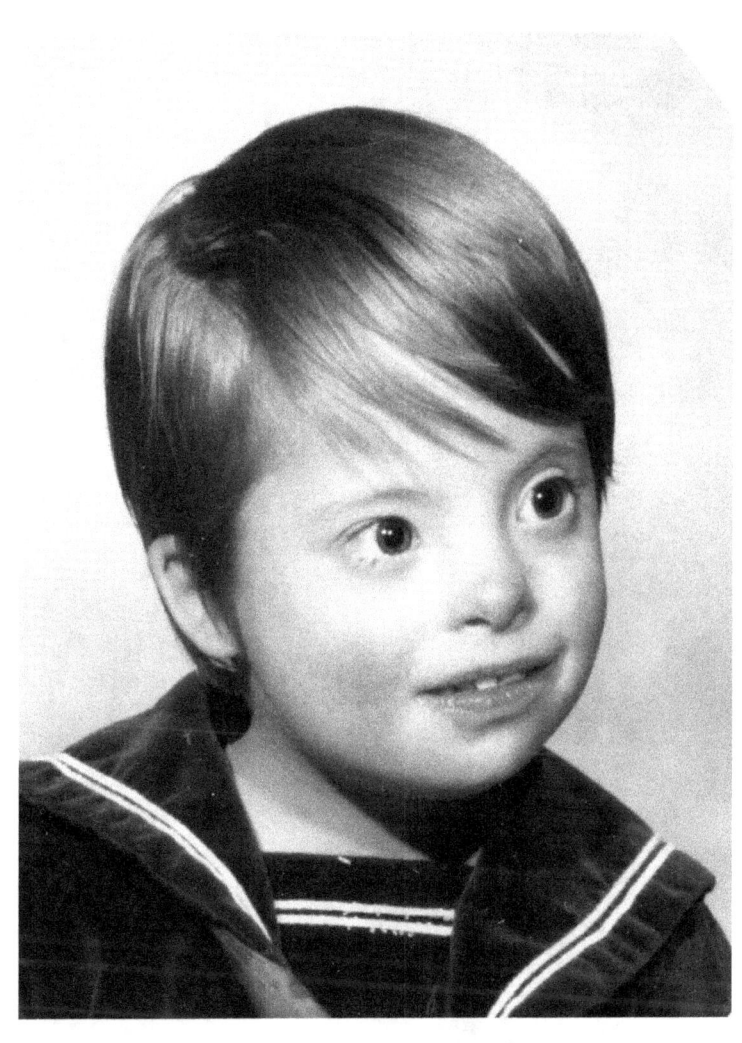

Jon 3 years old

Millie; with Grandpa Ami

Jon with Grandpa

*Old fashioned tin-type. No smiles allowed
Dick & Mark (back) Sondra holding Jon, Kristen,
Scott, David*

Dark Nights

5

MAY 22, 1975. The steady rhythm of Dick's breathing assured me he was asleep. *How could he fall asleep so quickly, so easily, on the most horrible of nights?* Clapping my hand across my mouth, I turned aside, stifling my cries. Oh, Jonny, hurry and come home.

It wasn't supposed to turn out this way. We'd worked so hard. Only several hours ago Dick and I had left our five-year-old son at the Utah State Training School for the handicapped, twenty miles away. Our family could visit Jonny next week, after his period of adjustment. He could come home starting the following weekend. Already my heart and empty arms ached for him.

The school was one of the country's most progressive. Increased federal grants and state funding enabled an average ratio of eight residents per teacher and daily sessions with a speech and physical therapist, psychologist and social worker. Periodic evaluations with psychiatrist, pediatrician and other medical personnel were scheduled as needed. Months before, I'd noticed Jon displaying occasional destructive behavior. I hoped his head-banging was just some passing anomaly, but the behavior slowly increased. Against window pane, floor, furniture, Jon began striking his forehead with terrible force. Heartbroken, I learned this was a typical self-stimulating behavior for brain damaged children. In turn, of course, it would likely increase damage if the behavior continued.

Through the long night amidst the cries of my heart I prayed for the success of concentrated behavior modification. To me the reason for Jon's admittance was the availability of qualified professional help—individualized for his specific needs, his improvement and return home. This was my hope.

For my husband, it was a different reason. Weeks earlier, Dick had broached the subject of Jon's placement at the state-run facility, feeling our little son's disabilities an ever increasing stress on the family.

"What are you saying?" I asked, incredulous. Stunned. *"You feel you and the children are being neglected?"*

"No, sweetheart. But you're not superhuman. Jon is getting harder and harder to handle. You're exhausted . . . and I'm saying we need to be open to the possibility."

No. Absolutely not. We'd get help. We'd do something. Anything. Except have Jon leave home. I would never consent to it!

Dick's words had been arrows piercing my mind and heart. Help us, Heavenly Father, I had prayed. Now, Jon was at the Training School and I lay beside Dick, devastated. My prayers continued, yet

Dark Nights

somewhere in my heart of hearts I felt it likely Jon would never again live at home.

After the initial conversation concerning the Training School, I looked at our family with honest eyes. I looked at our marriage; at Dick, Scott, Mark, Kristen and David individually.

Dick loved Jon with all his heart. He was a wonderful father to him. Difficult as it would be for Jon to leave home, Dick was prepared to make the decision he thought necessary. What I wanted was to continue on as we had, dealing with the challenges as best we could. I realized, nonetheless, I would *never* be 'ready' to let Jonny go.

Jonathan had special needs. In actuality, so did Dick, as did each of the children and myself as well. What was the delicate balance? Realistically, Jon's demands would increase. I only possessed so much energy, strength and time. As a wife, I needed and wanted to be by Dick's side. Our marriage—Dick's and my love for each other—was the bedrock of my life. I could not neglect our relationship. As a mother, I was primary care-giver, nurturer and teacher to *each* of my precious children. I could not jeopardize anyone's well being. But how could I be true to all?

I remembered the words of Jonathan's pediatrician, spoken when he was so tiny and his future so bright, brain damage unconfirmed. *Oh, Jonny. My sweet, dear, beloved Jonny, not yet six years old. You need me most of all.*

There was simply no equitable decision. Slowly, painfully, I

Dark Nights

began to acknowledge the Training School was a viable option. Perhaps the only option. *For now. Just for now.* I'd heard there was a long waiting list for admittance. There were no group homes at the time. No other facilities.

Within a few weeks I was able to bring myself to make an appointment for Dick and me to visit the school and become informed of its program. Perhaps Jon's head banging could actually stop or at least diminish. We met with the school's psychologist who interviewed prospective parents and guardians. I explained all we had done to help our little son reach his highest potential. I described his recent behavior patterns, our hope of his improvement and return home should we decide to admit him. "Jonny is currently attending preschool," I said.

After asking a number of questions, we were shown around the campus. Our hearts were wrenched as we encountered groups of severely disabled adult residents. Many were deformed. Many were in wheelchairs or were stumbling, barely ambulatory. Grunts—loud, repulsive noises exploded from some. Others were silent, their eyes vacant, disconnected. My heart welled with sorrow and compassion, yet also with aversion, I had to admit.

Shepherding the groups with nonchalance and aplomb, staff members smiled and nodded at us, somewhat easing our discomfort. From deep in the pit of my stomach the questions arose to my brain— *oh, Jonny, where will you be when you're old? How will you look? How will you act? Surely not like these.* My ensuing guilt could not

Dark Nights

wash away my sense of anxiety.

We arrived at the Self Help building, one of the newest structures, where children Jon's age lived. A tall, handsome man, Mike Snow, greeted us. The building supervisor, he appeared kindly and capable. We looked in the dormitory which was clean and neat. We peered in the classrooms. Children were busy in varied activities. Parts of their daily programming were similar to Jon's regimen from the Institute: sensory and tactile development; identification of colors, shapes, sizes; fine and gross motor exercises. I was favorably impressed.

Typically, conditions in our country's institutions had been deplorable. Neglect and indifference was rampant. Cases of abuse existed. Through the great labor of individual advocates, the Association for the Advancement of Retarded Citizens, enlightened educators and administrators—all believing the mentally handicapped capable of learning and progressing—perceptions began to change and conditions improve. Thereafter came the passage of Congressional law entitling all children, disabled alike, the right to education. School boards became involved. Recently dramatic change had taken place in our state's institution. I'm glad I was unaware of how bad things had been.

To target Jonny's self-stimulating behaviors, a specific program would be developed for him, a daily record kept of each behavioral act, adjustments or additional therapies introduced. Fair success with behavior modification was possible, we were told. We were also informed it could be a year or so before an opening for a child Jon's

Dark Nights

age became available.

If Jonny's head banging could be controlled, I now felt the Training School was the option. I had not discovered any other possibilities. What could be done in the meantime? Contact the Philadelphia Institute again and implement something? On my knees often, I importuned for divine guidance.

A week after our interview I received a phone call from the school psychologist. He had been touched by our visit, feeling our deep love and concern for Jonathan. He knew we were truly seeking what would be in his best interest, not placement for convenience. Because of our past efforts and because of Jonny's current needs, he had felt impressed to go before the admittance committee to strongly recommend adjustments be made for Jon's immediate acceptance. Jonathan could enter the school in five weeks.

It was not the door I wanted God to open. Open it He had. Of that I had no doubt. I offered heartfelt thanks. Still, on this first night with Jonny away, notwithstanding my deep gratitude, my heart ached with each beat. I lay beside my husband, tears sliding from my eyes, wondering throughout the interminable night how long it would take before it got easier.

∞∞∞

The hazy summer day we took Jon to school I'd packed clothes and toys, making sure his blanket and musical teddy weren't left

Dark Nights

behind. Jonny slept with them each night.

Dick and I met Jon's teacher, Kathy Terry, a lovely girl in her early twenties, with thick auburn hair, a sprinkle of freckles and beautiful hazel eyes. Jonny's family unit consisted of two little girls and now, with Jon, four boys. We stayed several hours, getting him settled. We watched him in class for a time. Curious, Jon was taking in his new surroundings, peers, and the activities.

Soon it was dinner time. Kathy took Jonny's hand and walked him to the dining room filled with half a dozen round tables and chairs just his size—bright pictures on the walls. We stood in the doorway, Jon paying us no attention. A good time to slip away.

The following day, my eyes on the clock, I made myself wait until late afternoon before calling. Each day inched by and I phoned for an update. Throughout the week Jon was being tested to evaluate his mental and physical level of performance. Between testing and classroom activities he was allowed, at times, to run about, investigating, which he thoroughly enjoyed. By experience, he was learning the rules and limits. "He sure knows how to test us," Kathy said one day, laughing.

Several times Jon had paused in the middle of doing something—his little lip protruding—and he'd begun to cry, obviously something triggering his memory about home and family. But he was kept busy and it was not a frequent occurrence. Night staff reported Jon was beginning to sleep through the night, not crying or climbing out of bed as at first. "He's really doing extremely well," Kathy assured me.

Dark Nights

Grateful for that, I also appreciated being made to feel comfortable in my calling every day. I could hardly wait to see him. To hold him.

∞∞∞

In seven more days we could bring Jonathan home for the weekend. Finally, the waiting over, we could visit. The children scrambled into the station wagon and we were off for the forty-five minute drive, anxious and excited.

The school was located in the small community of American Fork, 29 miles to the south. It lay atop a picturesque knoll which sloped away to other small communities. In the distance the long, silver strip of Utah Lake stretched below the line of the Oquirrh Mountains stacked on the horizon. On the east, the valley was bordered by the same towering, magnificent range as near our home. The buildings, old and new, were clustered on vast acreage, which in the institution's early days was cultivated to produce a food supply. Now, only a few acres were worked by adult residents to develop job skills. A small petting farm with a few animals remained.

The administration building, hospital unit, main kitchen, recreational building with its indoor swimming pool and maintenance buildings were interspersed between the residence buildings. Most of the units had their own small fenced yard, but a central play yard and park spaciously spread itself among the trees. Benches and several picnic tables were tucked here and there.

Dark Nights

Stepping into the Self Help building, my children craned to spot Jon. We checked in and Jon appeared. Kristen and David flew to him with hugs and kisses. Scott arrived, picked him up and threw him into the air, then twirled him about. Next, Mark pulled Jonny into his arms in a tight embrace. A stifled scream escaped Mark's lips as he jerked back his head. Jonny had bitten him on the cheek. Gingerly rubbing the bite, Mark said, "That's okay, Jon," instinctively understanding Jonny's growing excitement and joy had expressed itself in the most intense way possible, a bite rather than kiss.

Dick held his little son. Jonny looked into his face. Fast as a snake strikes, Jon's hand darted to Dick's forehead yanking off his glasses, something he'd not done for years. Jonny giggled and we tried holding our laughter, not wanting to encourage his behavior. Finally it was my turn. Kneeling down, I drew Jonny into my arms—filling them. Filling my heart. Jonny nuzzled his head into my neck. We held each other for a time.

Jonny smelled different. Surprisingly, that impression was the first thing to come to mind. *What was it?* Could it be possible Jon's body was absorbing the distinctive odor of the building? That was it. Oh, my.

I held Jonny's hand and we all walked a tour, finding Jonny's bed and locker. Outside, deciding to explore the large campus, we slipped into the car and drove about. We discovered a secluded, lovely spot, a small amphitheater of yellow-gold stonework arched over by a canopy of maple, cottonwood and ash leaves. Streaks of sunlight

Dark Nights

speared through the greenery. We spread out our picnic dinner and ate, the huge, august trees—tall pines among them—keeping us company. It became our favorite place when visiting.

Last, we spent a while in the play yard and it was time to go. In the dormitory, amidst a sea of brightly colored bedspreads, I undressed Jon and began pulling on his pajamas. He started to fuss, his agitation increasing.

"It's okay, Sweetheart. It's okay, Jonny," I crooned, trying to calm and comfort him. Dressed now, I wound the music box on his teddy and placed it, along with his blanket, into his arms. Together we rocked on the bed, back and forth. "Time to go nite-nite, Jonny." Understanding he was not coming home with us, Jonny began to scream, cinching his little arms about my neck. "It's all right, Sweetheart. You're okay, Jonny," I choked, trying to keep my tears at bay. The children fled the building, unable to bear the scene. Dick stood helplessly by. Louder and more frantically, Jonny cried.

Realizing it would only get worse I called to Kathy, who was undressing a child nearby. Agonizing with us, she'd been glancing over, wondering if she should offer help. "You'd better take him," I said. "Sorry." With Dick at my side, we rushed out.

Driving away, the car was silent as a tomb, each of us dealing with our own private grief. As we brushed away tears, sobs broke out despite brave efforts.

"He's going to be okay," I finally managed to say. "It's just going to take some time."

Dark Nights

Later, on my side of the bed, pain curled me into a ball and tore at my heart, a continuation of last week's night of despair. Had we done the right thing?

Yes . . . we had. A life-lesson whispered anew: Correct action and good decisions do not assure freedom from difficulty, pain or sorrow.

∞∞∞

After several months of coming home each weekend, Jonathan adjusted to the routine. Reconciled to school, he was not fretful when it was time to be driven back, and I managed to get through the week without deep, hollow loneliness. Our family settled in and life proceeded normally once again.

But Jonny was now a ward of the state. Dick and I were no longer his legal guardians. A technicality. Something to do with the state being able to receive federal funding. What his living at school meant to me, however, was that I no longer had full stewardship for his life. I could not be there for him, to hold him when he cried, reassure him when he was frightened or confused, or take care of him when he was sick. I couldn't be there to instinctively understand his need when others couldn't, and to comfort and love him. I was his mother, and though adjusting, I grieved.

Life Goes On

6

It was one of those mornings when the toast chars black, your child informs you he needs two dozen cookies, the car keys are missing—again—and the disposal clogs.

After the panicked key search and mad dash to buy goodies, with David late for school, I sat down to browse the classifieds. We were planning a remodeling project, but in the meantime we needed a couch. If I lucked out with a tolerable color, a used one would be fine—temporarily. We needed a six-footer. A seven-foot couch would be a touch too long to fit in the family room. *Moving: everything goes* one listing read, noting general items.

"Hello. I'm calling on your ad," I said. "I'm interested in your couch."

"Okay," a man replied, with his TV and children's loud clamor in the background. He'd misunderstood, thinking I had asked about his *cat.* The conversation continued.

"What color is it?"

Life Goes On

"It's whitish."

"Oh," I said, disappointed. "I was hoping for something darker. With children, I'm afraid it would get dirty too easily."

"We haven't had a problem. But it shampoos up real nice."

"Uh huh. What condition is it in?"

"Good."

"How old is it?"

"About two years."

"It doesn't have any worn spots, does it?"

" . . . Worn spots? Ah . . . no. No worn spots."

"What about the legs? They aren't wobbly or anything, are they?"

Another hesitation. "No . . . its legs are fine."

"Good. How much are you asking?"

"It's free."

"Free. Gee, I can't complain about that," I said, pleased. "What size is it?"

"Oh, average size," he answered, still thinking *cat*.

"Well, I really need to know the exact size. There's a particular place it needs to sit. I hate to bother you, but could you measure it?"

"Measure it. *You want me to measure it?*"

"Well, there's a chance it's too large. I'm sorry, but I'd sure appreciate it."

I heard unidentifiable words, then the clunk of the receiver as it was laid aside. After a time the voice returned. "It's sixteen inches."

"Ah . . . " My mind was working. "You mean sixteen inches

deep?" I didn't understand. "I need to know how long it is. Or rather, one might call the measurement 'wide'."

"Lady. *What in the world are you talking about?"*

∞∞∞

Humor gets us through many a clogged disposal and through the hard twists and knocks of life. Laughter heals.

One night as Fall breathed hoarfrost upon the ground, I reached for my electric blanket control, upping it several notches. No noticeable warmth came, so I turned it higher. Dick stirred, awake or fidgeting with some noxious dream, I couldn't tell. Still chilling, I turned the dial to high. Nothing. On the fritz I supposed. Too drowsy and too cold to muster myself out of bed for a blanket, I lay there with my goose bumps—miserable. Dick thrashed beside me. Suddenly, an *"Aaahhhhhaaaaa"* rent the air, startling me inches off the bed. "I'm so hot, I'm cooking." he panted. Somehow, in making up the bed, the controls got switched. He'd been turning me from low to off. We laughed, our laughter pealing down the musical scale an octave apart.

Life is like that sometimes—when the heat gets too hot. When pain and suffering feel too intense. When laughter *cannot* be found—anywhere. We wonder where God is. Yet, it's been said, "…the thermostat on the furnace of affliction will not have been set too high for us . . . our God is a refining God who has been tempering soul-steel for a very long time." [5]

Life Goes On

Clearly, though, there are times *I* turn the thermostat up. But what of 'innocent' suffering, not of my making, when I feel God is unmindful of the gauge on my furnace of affliction? When I knock on heaven's portal and it seems no one is home? And what of soul-steel? Can it ultimately be of the same refined eternal quality whether I've stoked the furnace or God's hand has set the thermostat? Innocence. Sin. Suffering. Redemption. Agency. Accountability. Grace. Mercy. The demands of justice. How do all the pieces fit?

∞∞∞

The concept of *God* is as varied and individual as we are, and how we perceive (experience) God in our minds and hearts remains singular to each of us. I respect your privilege to believe as you choose. Whatever our differences I trust we come together in our conviction that every life has meaning, dignity and purpose.

I believe for eons of time, before our mortal experience, we lived in a heavenly home as spirit children of Heavenly Parents. On earth, immediately after conception, we possess our entire genetic blueprint—the scaffolding of future physiological characteristics: eye and hair color, potential height, size and shape of nose and ears, etc. Our spirit and physical body unite to form our soul. Within us we also possess divine coding, 'spiritual genes' as it were, Godlike attributes: intelligence. Knowledge. Power. Spiritual alacrity and attunement. " .

. . trailing clouds of glory . . . we come from God." 6

From spirit come flashes of intuitive knowing—recognition—when an eternal truth *feels* right, for instance. Though mortality draws a veil over past life remembrance, our spirit retains its former knowledge.

My intent is not to present a specific theological tenet. Rather, I simply express what I believe. This belief helps me make sense of life. You retain your own perceptions.

If spirit is eternal in nature, to me it follows that life exists after physical death. To believe in God and life's purposefulness only to have life extinguished in finality of death, seems illogical. Sooner or later, my spirit returns to its Creator. What I have learned, what I have become remains integral, my only earthly possession checked at the border crossing and taken along.

I possess godly characteristics, a divine inheritance. However, unlike DNA, my spiritual blueprint is not fixed. Possessing agency, I have no blueprint guarantee. In other words, I can and do mess up, ears often un-tuned to my spirit and to God. Even when listening, I make mistakes. That's one way I learn, after all.

In the classroom of life, the laboratory of experience tutors my character one way or the other. Either I move from first grade toward a master's degree—toward greater knowledge, understanding, excellence, purity, mercy, charity—or I allow life's curriculum to suffocate my soul.

Sometimes I continually pick the wrong classes, or given repeated opportunity I keep flunking the exam. Yet always, the classroom remains open, and there is one Teacher I can count on.

However, I have to be willing to try, to work, to change, to take classes over, to clean up my messes on the laboratory table and to acknowledge, in the first place, that my messes exist. I have to scrub and scour with old-fashioned sorrow and repentance. When I've truly done my best, God renders the table spotless. I move a grade ahead, only to smudge up the lab once again and repeat the process. Yet, I'm making progress.

The good news is, I am not graded on the curve. I am graded against myself, and God knows what circumstances I was born into, and God knows my individual ability, and God knows my heart. Because I am His and He is mine, I have the capacity to pass the final exam with flying colors.

∞∞∞∞

Dick is driving our family home from visiting Mom Eva. Jonny has fallen asleep on my lap. David is sprawled-out in the rear of the station wagon. Scott, Mark and Kristen are sitting in the back seat.

"You're *touching* me!" Scott hisses at Mark, elbowing him in the ribs.

"Well, I beg your pardon, your Highness," Mark shoots back.

"A Highness is a woman."

"Actually, dear brother, the term is used for both male and female Royals."

"Be quiet you two, you're bugging me," Kristen says, disgusted. "You're always arguing."

"We are not," Mark replies, elbowing his sister in the ribs.

"*Ouchhhh.* Knock it off."

"Don't be such a baby."

"I'm not."

"Yep, you are."

Scott lets out a deep moan. Dick turns his head all the way around to the back seat. "All right! That's enough. Do I need to stop the car?"

This is not good. Well, not the possibility of the car stopping. This is *not* the time for eye-contact—whizzing down the street.

∞∞

The shoe store in Holladay was meticulous. Someone had spent hours stacking shoes into a tall cone-shaped display. Jonny sat on my lap in the store, an empty chair between the stack and us. "Oh, no you don't," I said. Knowing full well Jon's plans, I tightened my grip.

"May I help you?" a salesman asked. In that instant of distraction, Jon lunged into the display, shoes peppering the air. Oxfords. Penny loafers. Logger boots. Saddle shoes. Eyes turned as my 6 year old broke into gleeful laughter, shoes dropping to the floor one by one.

Earlier that week, Kathy Terry, Jon's teacher, had received the same astonished glances. With another co-worker Kathy had taken

Life Goes On

Jonny's family group on an outing to the zoo. Cresting a knoll by the polar bear exhibit, a woman had approached. With her children in tow, the mother held a sack of sandwiches. She'd placed the sandwiches into the original bread bag.

Jon recognized the bright Wonder Bread logo. *Food.* Off he ran, yards away before Kathy began pursuit. Kathy stretched her arm, her fingertips grazing the back of Jon's shirt. Up the pathway he sped, eluding her grasp.

Jonathan ripped away the woman's sack, sandwiches flying every which way. Kneeling on the asphalt, Jon began gulping down chunks of bread, taking no time to chew. In astonishment, as her mouth gaped open and her lips compressed into a line of disgust, the lady tossed her head and stalked off.

Kathy knelt beside Jon, salvaging what sandwiches remained. "Jon, shame on you." Herding the rest of the youngsters, the other teacher arrived, dropping down to help clean up. The two dared not look at each other lest they burst into giggles. Jon continued stuffing his mouth—hands darting to gather the dirt-covered fragments.

Tidying the mess, Kathy stepped up to the mortified woman, offering back the tattered bag of remaining sandwiches. Still in shock, the woman had not yet reasoned that *no* normal child, ill-mannered and out of control as he might be, would act so badly. Without scrutiny, Jon appeared to be a normal child. After an explanation, the lady graciously gave Jonny a pat on the head.

It was no happenstance that Kathy Terry became Jonathan's

teacher. I believe God placed her in our lives. She cared about all the children, but soon grew to particularly love Jon. Although Kathy was Jon's teacher for just a few short years, she remains my precious friend and Jonny's champion.

When Jonny was little, his looks and conduct did not appear unusual. As the years passed, our family received many a stare as people became aware of Jonny's disabilities and outlandish behavior. From the beginning, however, Jonathan's brothers and sister were never embarrassed or ashamed of him. Their hearts were filled with loyalty and protectiveness. Always, when I needed a hand with him, their hands were ready to help. They loved their brother dearly and fiercely.

Jon's smile and laughter, his mischievousness, his exuberance brought us continual delight and joy. It was a disheartening time when it became apparent he should no longer accompany us everywhere. Jon's loud noises and inappropriate behavior were becoming a disturbance. We expected Jon to be treated with dignity and respect. We, ourselves, had to proffer courtesy, respect and consideration to others. I particularly felt great sadness that Jon could no longer join us on most family outings. A precious era had closed.

∞∞∞

The Training School's evaluation placed Jon's mental and physical functioning at a varying level between nine months to two years of age. *Nine months.* Certainly this was an incorrect assessment. We knew Jon to be extremely perceptive, with a sense of humor beyond his years. He might feign insensibility, but he was a step ahead of us half the time.

The developmental program for the young children in Self Help, aptly, focused on self-help skills: toilet training, dressing, eating with utensils, responding to verbal instruction, etc. In addition, Jon's behavior modification program had been introduced. The reported number of head-banging incidents had decreased somewhat. *Oh Jon, will you be able to come home soon?*

One morning I received a call that Jon had gotten into some cleaning supplies, swallowing something. Fortunately, the fluid had not burned his mouth or esophagus, but he was being kept under observation in the hospital wing. Anxious, I drove down, parked and hurried along—my heels, like castanets, striking a rhythmic beat on the sidewalk.

"Hello," I said, passing a lone female resident. She grabbed my blouse, peering into my face with deep, misshapen eyes.

"Mama?" she asked—garbled but understood.

"I'm not your mama, but I love you," I said, taking her into my arms. How greatly relieved I was to be able to see *spirit* now rather than the distraction of physical appearance.

To my great comfort I found Jon perky and seemingly fine. Nonetheless, I spent the day with him. Later, stepping into the hallway for a drink, I saw a little girl lying in a reclining wheelchair.

She was three or four, perhaps, with severe hydrocephalus, her head huge for her tiny body.

She noticed me and looked up. Placing her little fingers beneath her eyes, she pulled her skin downward, widening her eyes, for the enlargement of her skull was beginning to block her vision.

Her vivid blue eyes could see me clearly now. With a blazing smile, she reached for my hand. I was overcome, humbled and unable to hold back tears. This little one, with delicate blonde curls, was a noble daughter of God. A spiritual giant, I somehow knew. I was privileged to be in her presence.

Summer Days

7

AUGUST, 1977. In the family room, with the stretch gates closed, I folded clothes while Jonny played on the floor. It had been a huge wash. Now the children could select what they wanted to pack for our upcoming trip. Kristen, nearly fourteen, was practicing the violin on the other end of the house. Hearing her play still amazed me. Five years earlier, Kristen had announced, "I want to start violin and join the school orchestra."

"Right," I'd said. "When I can't even beat you into practicing the piano."

"But, Mom. I really want to. I'll practice both."

I relented, expecting the phase to last a couple of months. Now, she was playing beautifully and taking private lessons from a notable teacher, Melba Lindsay Burton. Though the woman was elderly, they had become great friends. This morning Kristen had spent hours baking Mrs. Burton a birthday cake. My daughter, actually baking? I was bemused.

I stared at the row of unmatched socks despite my weekly search through bedroom closets and rummaging in the sack of singles. Perhaps I should lend credence to a Stocking Thief or cannibalistic washing machine. Jonny's music box had unwound. He threw it my way, just missing my shoulder. "Jonny. No." I said. "You'll hurt Mommy. Bring it to me, sweetheart. Don't throw."

I wound up the box. "Here. Come sit by Mom," I said, moving a stack of clothes. Jon stayed sprawled on the floor. Making a war whoop of sorts then giggling, Jonny grabbed a handful of building blocks and threw again. But not at me. "Jon. Don't throw," I said sternly, holding back a smile.

Jon was home for the weekend. At seven years he was still slender, but no longer tall for his age. In fact, he hadn't grown much. His gait had become increasingly unsteady, often causing him to stumble and fall. Jon's baby teeth had been knocked loose, coming out early and he was still head banging. With this problem and his tripping, he had a permanent lump on his forehead and a scarred lower lip. To me he still looked adorable.

"Well, if you won't come here, I'll come there," I said, finished with the clothes. I dropped down on the floor scooping him into my arms. "Wish you could come on our trip to California, Jon. And play in the ocean. I'll miss you so much, pumpkin." I kissed him on the neck before he wiggled away.

When Kristen appeared, I asked her to take her little brother to the bathroom. Walking Jonny through the kitchen, she tightly held both his wrists. Knowing he had spied Mrs. Burton's cake sitting on the

Summer Days

bar, Kris steered him aside. Jon removed his eyes from the temptation, acting oblivious. He was measuring his steps and true to form, at the appropriate second, he somehow broke free, shot out his arms and reaching up, plunged his hands into the double-decker. Kris let out an angry, horrified shriek. She couldn't stay mad for long, looking at Jon's cake-smeared toothless grin.

I helped Kristen clean up the disaster. "I'm so sorry, honey. You worked so hard. It was a real beauty."

"Yeah. Oh well," she sighed, wiping away a lingering tear of frustration. Plopping a disembodied hunk of cake into her mouth, she exclaimed, "Hmmm. Pretty good, if I say so myself." Words from childhood slid into my mind: *Don't waste. Starving children in Europe.* Promptly, I sliced each of us a huge, undamaged piece. Millie, by her spot at the side door, whined and licked her lips hopefully.

Out the kitchen window we caught a glimpse of David whizzing down the street on his bike, ready to swerve into our circular drive and fly up the bike ramp—catching air. Mark had helped him build the ramp. It was sturdy and strong. Even so, when I saw David coming I closed my eyes. Still at her spot and sensing it was David outside, Millie barked for a safe landing. I could look now and breathe again.

David had just turned eleven. Watching him several days earlier, I discovered how mature he was beginning to look. Slow down . . . and not just with riding your bike. Please don't you grow up so fast.

Summer Days

∞∞∞

Dick and I discussed how we'd celebrate our upcoming 20th wedding anniversary. With scheduling conflicts on the actual day, we'd do something special on the weekend.

October 25th arrived, with the usual rush to get kids off to school and Dick out-the-door to work. After the breakfast dishes were done and I'd raked up some leaves, I walked across our circular driveway to the mailbox. Millie was sniffing her way behind me, her nose to the ground.

Four advertisements. Two bills. A letter. I gasped at the return address. It was an anniversary card from friends who faithfully sent one each year. Dick and I had forgotten. No endearing words. No special hug. No lingering kiss. Nada.

Each anniversary, I received a dozen red roses from my sweet husband, one for each year of marriage—until the accumulating years proved too costly—then it was back to an even dozen.

I left the mail unopened. From our rose garden I picked one of the last remaining blooms of the season. The mail and lone rose, in its bud vase, sat on the desk in the kitchen alcove.

I honed up my acting skills as Dick arrived from work. "Hi, honey," I said as I gave him a hug and a peck on the cheek. "How was your day?" I glanced up at him with soulful eyes then quickly looked away.

"Fine," he answered, peering at me. "How was yours?"

"Fine." I stepped to the stove.

" Are you okay?" he asked, perplexed by my unresponsiveness.

"Of course. I'm good." I stirred the soup.

Dick shrugged, then picked up the mail. His face turned chalk white. He, too, immediately knew what was inside the envelope. "Oh, Honey. Oh, I'm so sorry," he cried as he rushed to me and took me in his arms. "I can't believe I forgot. Oh, I feel terrible."

"It's okay."

"I just can't believe it! Will you forgive me?"

"Don't feel bad. It's okay," I said, my eyes downcast.

"It's inexcusable," he apologized, hugging me tighter. Giggles spilled from my mouth. I'd tortured him long enough.

Another chance to use my acting skills came several weeks later. I was working on a surprise Christmas gift for Dick's office—a landscape oil painting. My oils were scattered on top of the kitchen table with my easel set-up next to it. The house smelled of turpentine, linseed oil and the paints. I held my palette, mixed the color I wanted, and squinted at the canvas. Out of the kitchen window, in my peripheral vision, I saw something. Good grief. It was Dick pulling into the driveway. Not *once* had he come home for lunch—in our entire married life. I froze for an instant, then grabbed my painting and fled into the bathroom.

Dick called, "Honey, where are you?"

"In the bathroom . . . ah . . . I am not feeling well." I hated to fib. "I have the stomach flu or something . . . and I think I might throw

Summer Days

up." I added more, "Can you fix you something to eat? Sorry, honey." I let out a realistic moan.

So much for the surprise—with paints strewn on the table and the house smelling like an art studio. However, on Christmas morning, my husband was indeed surprised. He had not noticed the smell or clutter.

∞∞∞

Behind the beachfront condo we'd rented for a week at Carlsbad, CA, the sun opened his eyelid on the water, dissolving grey into a hint of amber-rose. I was alone, the beat of the surf accompanying my soft-shoe routine. I'd awoken early, slipping out to practice my dance. The sand was cool beneath my bare feet. Two seagulls alighted nearby and cocked their eyes at me. "How does it look?" I asked.

I belonged to a quintet. Our singing group had been rehearsing a musical production for months, and our first performance was just weeks away. Finished with my dance, I dropped down, stretching out my legs. Planting my arms behind me, I leaned back, closed my eyes and breathed deeply the salt air.

Our family trip seemed to revive me. I'd been exhausted lately. As soon as our performances were over, I'd cut back, quit pushing, simplify and learn to say *no*. I'd rest up.

This was our last vacation together, the six of us, before Scott left for college. How could that be? My oldest ready to leave home. If I

Summer Days

reached out, it seemed I could pull my little Scottie into my arms. I'd feel a prickle on my cheek from his burr haircut. He'd be wearing Levis, a striped t-shirt and he'd sit on my lap and I'd read him a story.

Another of the precious stack of Galbraith family records stored sequentially in my heart. Whenever I chose I could play them. One by one, or randomly. Voice lessons. Songs to nourish my soul.

Typically the recordings would unveil ordinary moments—bedtime talks, piano practice, laughter at dinnertime, chats on the way to the orthodontist. Days colored with the commonplace, yet such moments were all the more treasured, sacred now in their simplicity. The days of our lives, forever past and gone, yet thankfully, available to pull to my mind.

As soon as we got home from our trip, I'd help Scott go through the closet he shared with Mark. One more time. A mother's ritual: sorting clothes, mending, passing on, giving away. Sorting toys. Evolution—stick-horse, cap gun, Tonka trucks to Hot Wheels race track and walkie talkies. Suddenly, no more toys stacked on the shelves. Instead, a radio and recorder sit on the desk, with a stack of tapes: Neil Diamond, The Dooby Brothers, Kansas, Bread, and Chicago. And car keys in the drawer.

Yesterday, I took you for your first walk, eleven days old, in a borrowed, ancient black leather buggy. Yesterday I nursed you. Wondered who you'd turn out to be . . .

I wiggled my feet into the sand, pulling my thoughts away. I wouldn't start saying good-bye. Not yet. But into my mind tumbled

Summer Days

images of the other children. Would this business of hacking at the apron strings get easier? No. For it would be saying good-bye to a different child, equally precious.

Mark was seventeen and into rock climbing. The shelves on his side of the closet had filled up with ropes, a harness, carabiners and pitons. For winter ice climbing there was a pair of crampons for his boots, several ice axes and a handful of screws. He was becoming proficient, scaling the sheer granite cliffs that walled-in several nearby canyons. "Don't worry, Mom. I'm cautious and don't attempt anything I can't handle." Well, he could break his neck tripping over a wastebasket, I supposed.

Mark, rather a Renaissance man, was still a tease. His temperament was the opposite of Scott's, yet they were close. They'd roomed together, always, and Mark would sorely miss his elder brother. Of course there had been arguments, raised voices and harassment along the way—even with Scott as peacemaker. Only once did the boys actually have a physical fight. Years earlier, from the dining room window, I had glimpsed them outside then watched in amazement as they lit into each other, fists flying. I was proud I hadn't rushed out, worried what the neighbors might think. It was their problem to resolve.

The sun had risen higher behind the beachfront condo, curling back the morning's shadow-line to meet my toes. The ocean strip was slowly coming to life. A sailboat. A pair of Frisbee players with their dog. A jogger, skirting the waves. Several adventurous swimmers

Summer Days

braved the cold before morning mists had cleared and the air warmed. Time to see if my sleepyheads were awake.

∞∞∞

Mark's arm is draped around Jon's shoulder as they rock back and forth in the tree swing. "Oh, look, Jonny. See the bird?" He points at the Magpie as it lands on the lilac bush, the iridescent blue of its feathers glistening in the sunlight. Jon rests his head against his brother's chest. Mark pats Jon's leg.

Kris comes out of the patio door, towel in hand. "Hey, Jon. Ready for a swim?" she asks, as she pulls him up.

"I'm heading back to school soon," Mark says as he gets up. He gives Kris a hug. "Tell Mom and Dad I said goodbye and I'll see you guys next weekend."

Kris helps steady Jon as they walk down the steps leading to the pool—where the old apple tree stood, supporting the tree hut. Where her brothers dug fox holes and raised pigeons. Inside the pool house, Kristen pulls an old Mae West life jacket from the cupboard, a left over from prior boating days at the cabin.

Jonny squirms as she ties him into the bulky orange vest. "The folks could splurge on a new one, eh, Jonny?" she grins. She helps Jon onto the diving board then guides him to the end. "Okay, here we go," she cries as she grabs a hold of him and, together, they plunge into the water.

Summer Days

Their heads pop above the surface, Jon's eyes wide. His arms cinch around his sister's neck, nearly choking her. She manages to dog paddle them to the side, hefts herself up, then pulls Jon onto the decking—his eyes still wide open. "Didn't mean to terrify you, Jonny," Kristen says, kissing his wet hair. Thinking things over, Jon begins to giggle. His giggles turn into boisterous laughter.

II
1977—2002

Both Jonny and my illness were dogged instructors. Finally, it occurred to me to ask, "Why was I sick? Was I responsible? What was really going on?"

Journey Resumes

8

AUGUST 31, 1977. The evening dress rehearsal for our musical production was in actuality a performance for all of our family members. It flowed without a hitch. I'd brushed away the exhaustion I'd been feeling lately, and reached deep within—getting the adrenaline flowing. With half a pint of 'grease paint' in my veins, I found joy and exhilaration in performing. It was especially delightful to glimpse my kids getting a kick out of their ol' mom, and Dick's look of endearment.

In bed, after an enjoyable mental review, I couldn't seem to relax—strangely hyper. I felt some sort of force gathering inside me. A prickly flush began washing down my body from head to foot. Like waves it came, every two or three minutes, and with it, a weakness I'd never known.

I fought down panic and a desire to wake Dick. I'd ride it out for a while, asking God to help me, to help remove my fear. Whatever was happening I knew one thing, I'd reached into reserves I didn't have.

Journey Resumes

Maybe I was coming down with some weird flu. Maybe low blood sugar was acting up again.

I'd lounge around the house and increase my protein intake. Surely I'd be fine for our first performance, a matinee four days away. I had to be. The show must go on.

I'll be fine. I'll be fine, I said over and over. After several hours, the frequency of flushing decreased and finally, toward morning, I fell asleep.

The day of our afternoon performance, I felt improved though not up to par. Afterwards, I crawled into bed, pleased the show had gone well. I'd be renewed by a good rest, I was sure. Our sextet had been practicing for months. We called ourselves, *Sugar and Spice*. We'd learned our songs, dance routines and lines, enjoying one another immensely. Our hard work had paid off. The audience responded with enthusiasm.

Alarmingly, the flushes began again. This was not some sort of fluke. I made a doctor's appointment. I'd be forty soon. Surely this wasn't some pre-menopausal thing—was it?

Back in college, I'd burned the candle at both ends and had begun feeling a lack of vitality and endurance. During the first years of marriage I often caught colds and flu, dragging around much of the time. I improved in time. However, several years ago my energy had dropped again, and a glucose tolerance test revealed extreme hypoglycemia. I was conscientious about my diet, sleep and exercise. Still, I was always tired.

Journey Resumes

I had been resting for hours since the show. I did not feel better. *What on earth was happening?* For one thing, I intuitively believed my adrenal glands were in a state of exhaustion, but I'd begun to develop another symptom besides the flushing. Heart palpitations. I didn't think them a result of anxiety, although I was having plenty of that.

I mustered the energy to get to the kitchen and took some specific nutritional supplements. I'd built up a little cache in my cupboard. At least I was doing *something* until my doctor got to the bottom of this. Back in bed I reached for my bible, and flipping pages, found the scripture I was after:

> *Fear thou not; for I am with thee: be not dismayed; for I am thy God: I will strengthen thee; yea, I will help thee; yea, I will uphold thee with the right hand of my righteousness.*
> Isaiah 41:10

I read it again and again, trying to keep a lid on my fear and concern.

It was a disconcerting, miserable sensation: the tiny particles of energy amassing and building, then a hot flush peppering my face. A throbbing, shuddering feeling would surge down my body. It seemed I could *hear* it as well as feel it.

Our singing group had two more performances this week. What in the world would we do? Well, the blend of their voices would be okay without me. Somehow, they'd have to pick up my solo and lines. My dance partner would need to improvise.

A number of shows were scheduled for the next month. Hopefully, I'd be up for the last of them. I dreaded informing the rest of the group who'd become good friends. What a disappointment. All those months of rehearsal, then this?

∞∞∞

"Your tests came back normal," my doctor said over the telephone.

"Well, I haven't had any more flushes. I still feel extremely weak. And I'm still having some palpitations. Where do we go from here?"

"Frankly, Mrs. Galbraith, I don't think I can be of help. I don't see anything physically wrong with you."

The implication was clear. My mouth dropped open in astonishment. "Well . . . ah . . . what do you suggest?" I stuttered.

"I don't have any suggestions." His words sliced through my ears like bits of cut glass.

"Ah . . . who do you recommend I see?"

"I really don't have any recommendations. I'm sorry."

That was it? I dropped the receiver into its cradle and burst into tears. I felt I'd been slapped in the face. Later, as I told Dick, the tears came again.

Within several weeks I had an appointment with Dr. Richard Cannon, head of endocrinology at a local hospital. "How your doctor acted was inexcusable." he said.

"Well, maybe I am a psychosomatic loony-bin," I laughed nervously.

"It's not in your head," he answered, smiling. "So let's find out what's going on." He couldn't have been sweeter or more solicitous. I came to out-patient for several days of extensive testing—draining, exhausting work. Checking on me, Dr. Cannon said, "I feel we'll discover adrenal involvement." His comment reaffirmed my budding intuition.

I was scheduled for a treadmill test—uncomfortable about taking it. But Dr. Cannon knew how weak I was. He was the doctor, after all.

As I lay resting one afternoon, I seemed to 'hear' a voice. Whether from my inner self or coming from a divine source, I knew not. *You are the steward of your body. You know your body better than anyone else. You have the right to personal revelation. Listen. Stand by your impressions, regardless of who might advise you otherwise.*

The first voice lesson of my illness was engraved in my mind. With trepidation I told Dr. Cannon I sensed I should not do the treadmill. "No problem," he replied. I'd stressed out for nothing but had learned a most valuable lesson: Believe in my inner voice.

Tests completed, I sat in consultation as Dr. Cannon briefed me. "I'm flabbergasted," he said. "I was sure there'd be adrenal implication and some other things showing up. But everything looks pretty good," he continued, shuffling through the results. "It's so frustrating to acknowledge we don't have all the answers. There's so much we don't know."

"Well, at least it's not all in my head. That's something, anyway. That is—*if you're sure.*"

"I certainly don't feel your problem is psychosomatic." He smiled again. "Something is going on, Sondra. I still think your endocrine system is involved in your symptoms, but I can't find anything definitive." Dr. Cannon leaned back in his chair. "I'm so sorry. All I can suggest is that you get a lot of rest. And slow down," he added.

∞∞∞

1978. The principle that diet and illness had a correlation to each other was not widely recognized when I grew up. Processed foods were thought the boon of progress. As a child, I was raised with a healthy lifestyle. Our family ate a variety of wholesome, unrefined foods, got proper exercise and rest, used no alcohol or tobacco, and we even took a few multi-vitamins and herbs here and there—long before they became common. We were ever so healthy. Through the years I'd kept up those helpful principles.

Here I was, though, struggling with health issues. I should have been flying high with such a beneficial foundation. My illness was heart-rending to my family. I continued to struggle—pulling back, redefining priorities—my energy and efforts centered on Dick and the children. I *couldn't* be sick. I needed to care for them.

Journey Resumes

Just when I'd think I was making progress, I'd crash, exhaustion siphoning my ability to do even the simplest of tasks: wash my hair, cook a meal, dust the furniture. I turned with greater emphasis to alternative healing where there was an offering of hope.

Over a year passed and I was getting worse. I spent most of my time resting. Okay. I could continue demanding more than my body could give, in spite of a lightened load, or I could come out of denial and admit I was truly a sick little girl; let go, allow myself to stay in bed and give my body a chance to regenerate.

All along I had prayed for strengthening, but also for God's will in my life. One day it occurred to me I might *not* get well. Never before had I considered such a thought. After calming down from the fear this thought triggered, I pondered my life.

I'd been exercising faith, doing all I knew to do physically and emotionally. Finally, I had quit fighting the reality of being ill. Nonetheless, I had only been giving lip service about God's will for me. I knew it. God knew it.

My life was in God's hands, whether or not I'd placed it there. What was God's will? At last, I surrendered myself—my life—to Him. Whether I lived or slowly ebbed away, I was in His charge. At last, I simply wanted what *He* wanted for me. This voice lesson filled my soul with sweet, comforting peace.

What I prayed for now, was that I would learn and grow throughout my illness and handle its challenges; that I would endure in patience, appreciative for blessings, healed or not. I prayed for my family that they too could endure well and grow from my illness.

I believe that God's grace is sufficient, after all one can do for himself or herself. Dick and I now faced a dilemma. Should we proceed with arrangements to see a doctor in California who prescribed drug therapy to patients with similar scenarios as mine? Wary, I'd have to be convinced of the therapy's safety. Also, the trip would be tremendously demanding—I hated even contemplating it. Knowing we were in great need of divine direction, we asked family and friends to join us in fasting and prayer.

Can a person receive personal revelation from God? If belief in God exists—surely one cannot question God's concern and love for His most precious creation. Would not a loving Father extend guidance to an importuning child?

Often, however, I am unaware when I've received divine help, protection and inspiration. Yet divine providence guides me throughout life, whether I'm paying attention or not. I might doubt, yet, with infinite tender mercy and kindness, God stands by me, offering His hand. Always.

A rare moment unfolded in my life, dramatically illuminating and charting the course of my future. *God spoke to my heart.* By the power and light of the spirit, I understood in a moment's time that it was God's will I be healed. This knowledge was laid before my mind, unequivocal and absolute. Confirmation blazed and anchored itself into my soul. I cannot attempt to explain or convince the verity of this sacred experience.

Journey Resumes

Astounded, I tried to take in the awe-filled message. *God's will is that I be healed.* Tears of joy washed away the sorrows and stress of the past. Despite all my weaknesses, all my faults and shortcomings, despite my messing up at the 'school laboratory table,' God *always* heard each heartfelt prayer I offered—this I'd always known. Now, to have this incomprehensible experience of *knowing,* it was simply miraculous.

Lifestyle

9

Let's get the show on the road. I expected to be up and about, daily increasing in strength. Instead, I could barely manage to shower and wash my hair every so often. Even talking seemed to exhaust me. Obviously, one lesson I was to learn concerned God's timing. Little did I know the cost of such a lesson.

Dick and I had the impression we should cancel the California appointment. Where we'd go from there we didn't know. I spent most of my days lying in bed now. "Maybe it's something in the water," I quipped, trying to figure out my feebleness and Dick's increase in headaches. The thought came to check the furnace. Yeah, sure.

"Lady, one more season and you'd have probably been in real trouble," the repairman said. Carbon monoxide had been leaking from a crack developing in the heating chamber of our gas furnace. The crack had become substantial. The furnace had been installed when we'd added our master bedroom suite years earlier. Likely, carbon monoxide had been present several years. Luckily our suite was separate from the children's bedrooms.

Lifestyle

∞∞∞

A dear and well-meaning friend of Dick's and mine offered his perception of my illness. He felt I had not adjusted to Jon's placement at school, that I was too focused on my little son. He believed Jon was the source of major stress in my life and had something major to do with my illness. His advice? We should not bring Jon home or go to visit him for a while. Also, I should seek counseling.

Immediately, I was on the defensive. *Not see Jon?* Now *that* would be a major source of stress, to say the least. I was dumbfounded.

It had been extremely difficult to place Jon at the Training School—as difficult as it would be for any mother having her five-year-old child leave home, normal or not. But I was a big girl, I said to myself. I'd worked through the adjustments. Certainly I'd have preferred to see and do more for Jon than I'd actually been able to do since becoming ill—just as I desired increased strength for my relationship with Dick and the other children.

Raising any child can be stressful, from swallowing a penny, to broken bones, to smashing up the family car. Certainly Jonny's challenges had been stressful, as had many situations with our other children. I did not believe, however, that Jonny's circumstances had been a significant source of my illness.

I felt I had good balance in acting on my limited energy supply.

Lifestyle

As long as I was able to be involved in Jon's life, measured as it was now, I felt content and peaceful concerning him. In my heart of hearts I felt Jon was not the issue.

Even so, a crack of vulnerability opened up. I began picking up little nuances drifting along the neighborhood grapevine. A friend repeated comments she'd heard. "If Sondra would just set her mind to it." "She ought to start jogging." "If she'd change her diet—she's a vegetarian, you know."

How dare they. What did they know? For one thing, I wasn't a vegetarian. If someone spied through our kitchen window they'd have known. Each time I'd attempt working into gentle exercise, the bottom dropped out. *Set my mind to it?*

What I didn't yet understand was that *I*, myself, allowed those perceptions into my life, allowed that type of negative energy and judgment. Most people were just trying to figure out why I'd been sick so long. They were interested and concerned. I would learn that what one feels—what one sends out—one gets in return. Life mirrors back my thoughts, intent and actions, showing me what works in my life and what needs changing. These are reflections, if I'm willing to look, willing to be honest.

I had not yet come to terms with my illness; guilty and apologetic for still being ill; unsure about my course of treatment; what was or was not appropriate for me. I was judging and criticizing *myself*.

Pondering the advice of Dick's and my friend, I let down my defensiveness and decided to see the psychiatrist he had

Lifestyle

recommended, a well known physician, Dr. Victor Cline. I needed to make sure I didn't have deep, subconscious issues about Jon.

The doctor said I was handling Jon's situation well, advising me to continue seeing and caring for him as I felt able. Up surged a feeling of great smugness. I was vindicated. Oh, how sweet the taste.

But I had been deflecting accountability for my feelings. Not so savory a taste after all. I alone was responsible for the way life's circumstances affected me, how I chose to experience them. If I had looked on myself with greater patience and charity, possessing confidence in my course of direction—throwing in a dose of lighthearted humor—I'd have viewed others in the same charitable light. Likely, most of the negativity wouldn't have been generated in the first place.

Assuming full stewardship and responsibility for my life was no easy task. I first had to understand what being 'responsible' meant. It would prove to be a slow journey, precept upon precept.

I came across a little book advocating the use of deep relaxation to still the mind and allow awareness of one's thoughts—*self talk*—to surface; discovering how thoughts shape and color one's reality. Thoughts actually creating reality! I'd never looked at life unfolding in this way. I was more surprised that I hadn't understood the concept sooner. What exactly *were* my thoughts? What was my self talk? My belief system?

Next, came the uncomfortable question: *In what way was I responsible for my illness?* Was I willing to take a look to discover possible reasons or influences? I took a deep breath. I was. Yet it would take time, effort and a developing expertise to find answers.

Since my illness, I'd often brought comforting, encouraging words to mind—wanting love and light to fill me. However, I now saw a concrete, rich new vista: the mind-body connection, the power of the mind to heal through meditation, affirmation and visualization. I could now broaden the scope and the application of principles I'd already been using.

With great interest and curiosity I began paying attention to my thoughts, more aware that thoughts precede feelings. I had to acknowledge I alone was responsible for how I felt and acted. No person or circumstance could make me react in a certain way. If I say, "This makes me so frustrated," or "You make me so mad," it just doesn't fly. I am free to choose my responses. It's hard work governing myself, acting, not reacting. I am a creature of habit—I had habits to break. Inching along, I worked to acknowledge my feelings without judgment or criticism and accompanying guilt.

I had the good fortune of having a Mother who was kind and patient. She was consistent and optimistic in nature. I don't remember Mother getting angry. I never heard her speak ill of anyone. Rather, she focused on the good in every person and the good in every circumstance. Mom was basically a happy person.

It sounds as if my Mother was a *saint*. I thought she was. In those earlier days, concerns and personal matters were kept private. Certainly, mother faced issues, but I was unaware of them. It is not easy living in the shadow of the saintly.

By Mom's example and nurturing, I developed, for the most part, a confident and positive outlook on life. Nonetheless, with such 'perfection' before me, I developed a misconception. I equated bad feelings with *being* bad. No one ever told me it was okay to feel angry, resentful, jealous or sad. By her demeanor, Mom never showed me that negative emotions were a part and parcel of life. When I did experience them, I tucked them away—afraid and guilty.

All feelings need to be acknowledged and validated, whether or not they are justified or even true. Feelings simply 'are.' I honor myself by owning my feelings. Then, the great endeavor begins: acting responsibly on my feelings; peeling back layers to reveal the core issue that created them in the first place; taking an honest look; choosing to change perceptions. Surely Mom had experienced her share of negativity. She habitually chose to govern such feelings with charity and forgiveness, for herself and others. I just missed a step along the way.

I had to be ever so gentle with myself as I learned to allow all my feelings. I did not yet comprehend my issue with perfectionism, which would unfold several years later in a shocking revelation.

Meantime, I focused on increasing my awareness, on learning to still my mind and becoming *centered* and *grounded*. This was new terminology for me. I focused on filling my mind and body with peace and well-being, on visualizing health, affirming health, and claiming health. I focused on picturing my body slowly healing day

Lifestyle

by day.

*

Another principle was at work, even though my conceptual understanding would come later. When a person's intent is to learn, to grow, when a person is willing to change, to receive of life's abundance, life provides *teachers*—learning experiences—enabling one to move forward.

My son Scott met a woman, Barbara, who'd experienced symptoms similar to mine. She had made marked improvement from some sort of treatment. Did I want to talk to her? Of course.

From a phone conversation with Barbara, I learned about the Clinical Ecology Unit at the American International Hospital in Zion, Illinois. The clinic was run by Dr. Theron Randolph, M.D., who was considered the pioneer physician of Environmental Illness and also known for his unique approach in food allergy treatment.

Barbara sent an information packet from Dr. Randolph's clinic. I was already aware that pollutants and toxic chemicals exist in our environment. I knew chemicals enter our body through skin absorption, from items we handle, through air we breathe, from water we drink and from food we eat—containing pesticide and herbicide residue, additives and so forth. However, I was woefully uninformed concerning the *magnitude* of harmful exposures that our bodies encounter and the devastating effect of these exposures on susceptible persons. Me?

As I read the packet I became convinced that a significant

component of my illness was a weakened immune system, a result of myriad chemical exposures. Outdoor pollution, certainly, but I had not considered indoor pollution. In the quest for energy efficient homes, to reduce the cost of heating and air conditioning, we seal ourselves up with chemicals that are released into the air—called 'outgassing' (containers don't have to be open for products to outgas).

I thought about the pungent smell of our new carpet; the potent oven cleaners and insect sprays I'd used; my fingernail polish; the 'plastic' smell of my shower curtain when it was new.

Over time, a person's immune system may become compromised, without one's conscious awareness. A significant chemical encounter might take a person's immune system over the edge. Once damaged, the body's defense mechanism is most difficult to heal. Immune dysfunction opens the door to a host of illnesses.

I had an episode of lead poisoning as a child. Could toxic metal poisoning that long ago still be affecting my body? I also absorbed mercury while working for a dentist. And had I sustained damage from the recent carbon monoxide poisoning from our furnace?

Dr. Randolph discussed the seriousness of food allergies in sensitive individuals. I was certainly aware of rare, life-threatening reactions (someone nearly dying from eating shellfish or peanut products, for instance) but developing fatigue, pain, swelling, diarrhea, eczema, hives, migraines—a host of other symptoms because of a *food allergy*?

Lifestyle

After food testing and the elimination of offending foods from the diet, Dr. Randolph advocated a Rotation Diet, eating 'safe' foods once every fourth day. The foods we eat most often are usually the troublesome ones. I glanced at the list of foods containing corn—as in corn sugar, corn syrup, cornstarch, etc. Good grief.

I pondered the Food Allergy and Chemical Sensitivity information. How careful I needed be around chemicals to safeguard my health. Not only that, I bear an individual responsibility to protect and preserve our precious, fragile environment.

I mulled over the protocol Dr. Randolph recommended: For individuals experiencing toxic chemical overload, it was not a matter of using common sense precautions and good judgment in handling chemicals (wearing gloves and a mask, for instance), or even decreasing the use of chemicals and finding safer alternatives. *It was a matter of avoiding their use altogether.*

Dr. Randolph mandated the establishment of a safe room—stripped of all synthetic materials and items suspected of outgassing—a safe haven where a person's body, free from exposures, could begin to recover, as he or she also followed the rotation diet.

I'd have to undergo a complete change in lifestyle, my family as well. I couldn't begin to fathom the discipline and commitment required. As I worked through my frustrations, excitement grew. I definitely had been handed pieces to the puzzle of my illness. Yes. I would schedule myself at the clinic, a four-month's wait. A phone

Lifestyle

call came. There had been a cancellation. Could I come in two months?

Farewell

10

Before my trip to Illinois, our family used the time in preparation. I ordered a custom-made 100% cotton mattress without fire retardant and purchased 100% cotton clothing. No more synthetic fabrics for me. Cupboards and closets were cleaned and unhealthy items thrown out or given away. Dick and the children converted the master bedroom into my 'safe room' where I'd spend the majority of time for several months, giving my body a chance to heal.

The synthetic carpet, drapes and an overstuffed chair were removed along with much clothing and nearly all my cosmetics. I sorted Dick's toiletries too. A lone bottle of unscented shampoo, unscented lotion and a cake of Neutrogena bar soap now sat in my ransacked vanity. Dick's cupboards looked equally meager.

From our attached garage, Dick sorted paints, insecticides, oils, etc., putting what we'd keep in a separate shed, no chance for fumes to seep inside. I ordered an air filter, natural cleaning supplies and detergent, then set up delivery for bottled water. We were amazed our house had been filled with so many outgassing chemicals.

Farewell

∞∞∞

How would I manage the flight back east? I thought about my few trips outside the house—being driven to the doctor's, lying in the back seat of our car too weak to sit up, watching tops of trees. Watching telephone wires in an undulating flow, converging to the next pole, then zinging apart again. Lying there—watching—wanting help but simply wishing to be back in bed, exhaustion draining away my life. I faced the upcoming trip with a mixture of dread and great hopefulness.

Dick checked me into the hospital in Illinois. We spent a few precious minutes on a lovely deck overlooking a stretch of thick trees. Then he had to leave. No visitors were allowed into the unit itself where all personnel, doctors and patients were required to wear natural fabric clothing and use non-scented toiletries. My husband held me a very long time. Soon he was gone and vanishing with him a measure of my strength, the source of my comfort. I stayed on the veranda until I gained composure and my tears dried.

After an initial fast to clear the system, all patients were served one food item per meal. Each patient kept a record of pulse rate, blood sugar, etc. and symptoms were carefully notated. I was amazed that I reacted to so many foods common in my diet. I experienced nausea, dizziness, heart palpitations, headache, nervousness, fatigue, joint pain. One woman's reaction triggered a dramatic personality

Farewell

change—belligerence, aggressiveness and hostility. After fasting, several arthritis sufferers became pain free only to have certain foods cause an immediate return of stiffness and pain. We patients became believers that food allergy was a legitimate health issue.

Testing revealed I did *indeed* have extreme chemical sensitivity, especially to hydro/petro-carbons (of which everything in our modern world seems to be made.) Inside a sealed booth, while tested on natural gas, I became violently ill. What an eye-opener.

Patients attended classes, learning about the physiology of food and chemical allergy response. We were given tips on avoiding exposures, given handouts on product information, a suggested reading list and pointers on how to emotionally deal with this illusive illness.

Terribly lonesome for Dick and the kids, I remained at the clinic nearly a month. [7] (It took that long to pass enough foods to rotate when I arrived back home.)

I came home armed with knowledge, but overwhelmed. I was terribly skinny, too, yet determined to continue with my rotation diet and staying put in my environmentally safe room. Gradually, I grew stronger and stronger. Finally, I was on my way. I also continued my mental programming. *I am healing. I can get on with life. Hallelujah. Hallelujah.*

After several months I ventured into the world, my immune system more vital, my body able to neutralize and detoxify pollutants. I could stay up later. Go a few places with Dick. We tasted a

Farewell

semblance of normal existence after two difficult years. Oh, how deliciously sweet. We held hands in an early movie. We laughed over lunch. We took tiny walks, arms linked around each other's waists.

With Scott and now Mark on their own, we had only Kris, David and Jon to join us on outings to the cabin. On a lovely weekend trip with the three children, it seemed like old times being at our beautiful valley home. Light was shining again in my husband's eyes. "I've got my Sonie back," he said.

Several months later, whether I'd pushed too hard or some piece to the puzzle was still missing, *I came crashing down.* Dick's disappointment sliced deeper than mine. Of all the vexations of my illness, not having me by his side was the most difficult. There was nothing to do except for me to pull back, regroup and reevaluate.

∞∞∞

JULY, 1979. We were at our valley home for the 4th of July holiday weekend. I rested on the shaded patio, Millie lying beside me, panting with the heat. The rest of the family was off boating. The horses grazed together under the giant cottonwoods down by the stream. How we missed our old Appaloosa, Topaz. Going lame, he'd had to be put down.

Millie sat up and stuck her nose under the palm of my hand, wanting a pet. "Just me and you, Mil," I sighed. I longed to be at my folks' house. My siblings were gathered there with Dad and Mom. I

Farewell

should be there, too. *This lousy illness of mine.* Only twice during the last several weeks had I felt strong enough to be with my family, just to visit, not having the strength to be of help. At least I'd managed to join them and have us all together—to say good-bye to Dad before he passed away. Father was gravely ill but had wanted nothing to do with the hospital. So he remained home.

My father, Ami Lorenzo Richardson was eighty-four now and recently so active. He'd been finishing off a bathroom in the basement. We thought he'd go on forever. In 1963, when Mom and Dad moved to Utah, Dick and I were thrilled. I'd had no extended family living near.

My parents were tremendously generous and helpful to *all* their children—babysitting grandchildren, working on home improvement projects, forever doing something. It was wonderful to be able to have them for Sunday dinner, along with Dick's mother. They also joined us for most holidays and special family occasions. The years were a treasure.

Dad was born in 1894, catching the winding down scenes of the century, the fading sun of the untamed west: buckboard. Hand plow. One-room school house. Outside privies. Cattle rustlers. Horse thieves. Diphtheria. Whooping cough. Born of hardy pioneer stock, he lived as he'd been taught: a life of industry, flawless integrity and principle.

In 1918, my father sailed the rough Atlantic seas in the belly of a troop ship, arriving in France shortly before the World War I

Farewell

armistice was signed, fortunately seeing no front-line action.

When Dad had become ill, I called my brothers and sister. As Dad worsened, Jay, the oldest, came from South Dakota for several weeks between semester break at the university where he taught. Later, my siblings Vel Dean, Fran and Gary arrived from southern California. We spent precious hours crying, laughing and telling stories. Escapades were retold, embellished perhaps, part of family lore now.

One afternoon, with the summer sky a cornflower blue, Dick and I took Mark, Kristen and David to see their grandfather—driving the familiar route past the majestic State Capitol which overlooked the city and on up the steep tree-lined street of DeSoto. DeSoto, where our kids had played and trick-or-treated at Halloween and had eaten scrumptious homemade whole wheat waffles. It was the children's last farewell to the noble grandfather they so deeply adored and admired.

Mark had come home that day from college, a city away. Scott was out of state and received a phone call from DeSoto. With the receiver held against Dad's ear, he and Scott shared a few precious, final words as the rest of us wept. Concerned that Jonathan would be too hyperactive, we hadn't brought him along. How I wished Jonny could also be with us to have one last hug. One last fingering of Grandpa's mustache. One last song.

Each of us siblings had spent time alone with Dad while he was strong enough to talk. Private, tender moments. Kneeling beside the

Farewell

sofa one day I gently stroked Dad's hair, still not fully grey. I laced my fingers through his fingers, kissed his cheek then laid my head on his shoulder. "I love you, Daddy."

With effort he whispered, "I love you, sweetheart."

"I could never have had a more wonderful father than you," I said. Feelings rather than actual words conveyed the treasure stored in our hearts. His voice, though silent, was eloquent. Nourishing.

Dad gave my brothers Francis and Gary a father's blessing. He counseled, encouraged and praised his sons. Since Jay had returned to South Dakota to teach summer quarter, dad taped a blessing for him before consciousness gently faded from his eyes. Jay was expected to arrive in a few hours, while I pined away here at the cabin.

Sensing my melancholy, Millie sat up and gave a low guttural whine. I gave her a reassuring pet and stroked her for a time. Content now, she laid back down beside me. We watched the horses plod single file from under the cottonwoods, headed to the pasture to graze.

My siblings would be visiting now—Vel, Fran and Gary comforting Mom while they kept vigil over death. Ami could linger days longer, the doctor had said. I had no strength to stay with him. Feeling helpless, Dick and I had decided to come spend the weekend at the cabin to ease the waiting.

Dick and the children returned from boating. In bed by late afternoon, I lay awake into the night. I heard the phone ring downstairs, and knew. After Jay had arrived, the family gathered

Farewell

around Dad's bedside while Jay listened to his blessing on the tape recorder. Minutes afterward, Daddy was gone. Memories kept me company throughout the night.

LOS ANGELES, CALIFORNIA—1944

Our home on Panorama Terrace was anchored upon a steep hillside which flowed down into the Los Angeles basin. Hollywood was several miles due west. On a clear day, from our back balconies we could see all the way to Santa Monica—the ocean a thin strip of grey-blue.

A large floral print easy chair sat in our living room. I often sat on Mother's lap in that cozy chair, as she read to me in her wonderful, expressive voice.

One Christmas, Dad pulled the chair to the fireplace. We snuggled in. He wrapped his arms around me as we watched flames chew at the fragrant logs—five of us kids' long red Christmas stockings backlit on the fireplace screen. Tree lights and fire glowed. I tried to stay awake, there in the comfort of Dad's arms—love and Christmas dreams closing my eyelids.

There must still be a tiny echo of our voices, our laughter ringing in those hills where we grew up—Jay, Vel, Fran, Gary and me. Where we played kick-the-can, follow the leader and hide 'n' seek; in a day when childhood was

Farewell

filled with innocence. It seems our voices still ring there, where I climbed trees and skinned my knees, where I played marbles, jacks and hopscotch; where I roller skated and played soldier.

War raged in Europe and the Pacific. I was too young to understand its unspeakable horrors. Naively, I thought the whole affair rather romantic, patriotism swelling in my breast as love and pride for my country deepened. I thrilled when I saw those heroic soldiers and sailors, all so handsome, so dashing in their dress uniforms. They swarmed the city streets, on leave from nearby bases.

The fighting was far away. I felt no fear, even though we practiced city black-outs and air-raid drills at school. In class, we'd crawl under our desks, covering our arms over our heads, or file to the basement where we'd sit—lined against the halls—wrapped in a blanket we'd brought from home. Silent as gnomes.

We had a Victory Garden at school with our scarecrow, Uncle Wiggly, watching over us. I did my part for the war effort—saving string. A fist-sized ball sat in my drawer, growing larger and larger, along with a ball of foil, meticulously peeled from gum and candy wrappers. Every so often, I'd turn the balls in at our corner grocery. I'd get a

Farewell

pat on the head and a few cents.

Gas rationing and food stamps were mandated. The only thing bothering me were holes in my shoes. We little Americans had to 'make-do' as leather and rubber were needed for combat boots. We'd trace our soles over cardboard, then stuff the cardboard liner inside our shoes—which lasted five minutes.

"Mama," I said, "I hate these crummy, ratty old shoes. They make me feel ugly."

"Just keep wearing your beautiful smile. People will notice your face, not your feet."

Other voices touched my soul during those years; voices on the radio and on the movie newsreels. Helen Keller was difficult to understand, nonetheless she spoke clearly to my heart. Mahatma Gandhi, his fasts, his thin bare-chested body sitting cross-legged on the ground—his actions of nonviolence, spoke more articulately and powerfully than his actual words. Winston Churchill—his impassioned voice an ocean away—thrilled me through the noisy static.

> "*We shall not flag or fail. We shall go on to the end . . . We shall fight in the sea and oceans . . . We shall fight on the beaches, we shall fight on the landing-grounds, we*

Farewell

SHALL FIGHT IN THE FIELDS AND ON THE STREETS, WE SHALL FIGHT IN THE HILLS; WE SHALL NEVER SURRENDER . . ." [8]

Hitler, with his high-pitched ravings, was a study in contrast. Though we knew him to be deadly, he seemed nearly comical, goose-stepping in his shiny long black boots. We'd mimic and ridicule him, and sing a song, thrusting up our arm in a German salute and making a *raspberry* with our tongues at appropriate spots:

Ven der Fuhrer says
Ve is der master race,
We'll hail (pssstttt) hail (pssstttt)
Right in the Fuhrer's face.

Ven der Fuhrer says
De'le never bomb dis place,
We'll hail (pssstttt) hail (pssstttt)
Right in the Fuhrer's face. [9]

After a long day's work, Dad enjoyed having me comb his hair. It was a form of relaxation to him. He'd pay me ten cents. Dad, with his mustache, looked like Hitler when I combed his hair straight down over the side of his forehead. After a fiendish makeover, I'd shudder in delightful terror.

Farewell

ONE NIGHT, I AWOKE TO WHAT I THOUGHT WAS THUNDER. IT WASN'T. ON OUR BALCONY, DAD'S ARMS HELD ME TIGHT AS MY PARENTS AND I WATCHED THE BURST OF ANTI-AIRCRAFT GUNS, EXPLODING LIKE FIREWORKS INTO THE SKY. FOR YEARS, ARTILLERY HAD BEEN IN PLACE ALONG THE BEACHFRONT.

WE COULD FEEL THE REVERBERATING PERCUSSION AS EACH GUN DETONATED. POWERFUL SEARCH LIGHTS PROBED THE NIGHT, THEIR BEAMS CRISSCROSSING THE SKY—THE HORIZON LIGHT AS DAY. WITHIN THE SAFETY OF MY FATHER'S ARMS, I WATCHED IN FASCINATION. THE NEXT DAY THE NEWSPAPER AND RADIO OUTLETS COVERED THE INCIDENT, BUT HAD BEEN STONE-WALLED. NOTHING DEFINITIVE WAS REVEALED BY THE GOVERNMENT. SPECULATION ABOUNDED THAT EITHER OUR MILITARY ACCIDENTLY SHOT AT OUR OWN PLANES, OR JAPANESE PLANES MADE IT TO OUR SHORES.

∞∞∞

After receiving the phone call about my father's death, bittersweet emotions pulsed through the hours, laying bare my heart. Memories floated, adrift, through wakefulness and in my dreams.

I remembered that night on the balcony during the war. I remembered the feelings of security and peace within my father's arms.

I heard my father's voice sounding its way through hazy layers,

Farewell

clear as I became fully awake. "Hello, half-pint." "How's my pumpkin?" "My little Sonie."

I'd never grown too old to want his hugs. His love. *Oh, Daddy, Daddy.*

Send Off

11

JUNE 10, 1981. I am alone. Dick and Scott will be boarding the plane about now for Scott's marriage in Arizona. I gently rock our backyard tree swing, taking in the beauty around me. Flowers are in bloom. The mountainsides have turned from winter brown to lush green, yet a few snow-capped peaks remain. A robin lands and chirps a cheery song.

I have not given myself the usual pep talk—pulling myself up by my bootstraps. Without conscious effort I feel a particular serenity. I realize my feelings are being influenced, bearing a tender message: *I've heard. I understand. I care.*

How I'd prayed to God that I would be strong enough to attend Scott's wedding. I had even packed my bags. At college, Scott met a cute little blonde with gorgeous blue eyes, his date's roommate from Phoenix. Tomorrow she will become Glory Galbraith. Glory is lovely and down to earth. We are all so very pleased that she is becoming a member of our family!

Send Off

Riding with several of Scott's close friends, the other children have arrived safely in Arizona. A few hours ago, with Scott holding his breath, Dick and I had waited until the last minute before deciding that I should not attend. I simply am not well enough to handle the trip.

From atop the bed where I'd been resting, I had stepped to my eldest child. I placed my hands on the sides of his face and gazed at him. Sun streamed through the glass doors, lighting Scott's eyes—one bright blue, the other deep brown. Almost startled, I realized I had not paid attention to his eyes' uniqueness for years.

Failing to hold back tears, we embraced. No words were necessary but we managed a few. How I will miss him, this son, no longer mine; a man now, ready and capable to start his own family unit with Glory.

∞∞∞

How could I so quickly let go of the peaceful feelings I had—after Dick and Scott left for the airport? I know I experienced God's loving comfort and encouragement. *Yet, I should be at the wedding today.* Here I am, still like an old horse run too far. Collapsed. Done-in. I've worked so hard to get well. I've learned. I've grown. I know God is mindful of me, but I'm so tired of all this. *What's happened to the promise? What's happened to His will that I be healed?*

What more can I do? Re-evaluate, yet again? One thing has

Send Off

occurred to me, buzzing into my head: Our home has radiant heat. There is no air-flow to filter and purify. With increased traffic, the air quality in our neighborhood has decreased. Do we need to consider moving? Surely it won't come to that.

∞∞∞

NOVEMBER 1981. I stand at the doorway taking one last look. Outside the large picture window, past the patio and my dear rose bushes, past the branches of the grand old Ash tree and on past the slope, the mountains are a faint snow line through the haze. I take in the living room, the dining room—two steps up, the kitchen to my left, with cafe doors that noisily clack back and forth on tight spring hinges. The doors block the kitchen nook from my view, the cozy nook where years of conversation and laughter nourished our souls as surely as food nourished our bodies.

I take a last look down the hallway to the rooms where we all slept. Empty. Everything is loaded now except my bed, which is being disassembled. In our new house the bed in the guest bedroom is already made up for me. I will stay there, within the guest room's unpainted walls, until the master bedroom has time to 'gas out.'

I lift my hand to touch the wall. Voices are resonating, held there: A child's laughter. Whispered secrets. The faint pulsing of dreams. Hopes. Tears. I can feel it *all,* the walls filled fifteen years full.

Send Off

Through this door I carried little David, three months old, Kristen holding my hand. Here David rolled on the floor with Millie, just a pup, long before he could walk. Here Scott and Mark chased, and Dick and I slept in on Saturday mornings far away from the chatter of early weekend cartoons. Here Scott practiced the piano and Mark fashioned cardboard marvels for the little ones. Here, Mom, Dad and Mother Eva lounged on Sunday afternoons.

Through the side door, I carried Jonny—tiny, safe and loved. In these rooms, pitch black, we played hide-n-seek, still as mice, our hearts beating wildly. Here, we spent Monday evenings, just our family, gathered together for time alone.

Outside, we shot baskets, tossed the football and built snowmen. Within these walls Dick and I watched our children grow—and leave.

Our dear, dear, blessed home. One more glance—memories spilling over like my tears—and then I step out, never to return. Except in my dreams.

∞∞∞

Grunts and groans ebbed and flowed along the hallway outside the guestroom door, as Dick and the kids continued unloading. I wanted to be part of the excitement, the work, but I had to stay put.

The newlyweds, Scott and Glory, lived in town where Scott was attending the local university. Mark was now living at home attending the same alma mater. David, his brothers and Kris and Glory were helping with the move, along with Kristen's boyfriend, Marv. Later,

Send Off

Mom Eva would come to help set-up the kitchen.

We'd built a new home in Sandy, a suburb southeast of our Holladay home. Of all the outlying communities, the air quality was exceptionally good. Our three-acre lot was spread along the foothills. Houses lay higher on the mountainside, but from our lot none were visible. It seemed our backyard flowed, breathtakingly, straight up the slope to the sheer granite cliffs. Scenic Little Cottonwood Canyon yawned open its mouth just minutes away. Rock climbers flocked there. Mark was happy.

Through the summer months, Dick and the boys had built a barn—second time around—and fenced in the property. We planned to occasionally bring the horses down from The Valley.

In the neighborhood there were still wide open spaces. We could hear rosters crow. It was a quiet, pristine area where my body could heal. We'd built our house with the safest materials available, selecting brands of plywood, insulation, etc., that met high environmental standards. Water-based paints were used. We had old-fashioned plaster walls, tile and wood floors, and one hundred percent wool carpets with old-fashioned horse-hair pads.

From the busy hallway heads popped in occasionally. "Where does this go?" "Where should we put this?" I lay there, trying to believe we were actually in our new home. Millie must feel lost, I thought. She was old and feeble now. Dear, sweet Millie. Was she huddled in some corner watching the confusion? I wished someone had time to bring her to me.

Send Off

In the early evening, I slipped out, taking a short main-level tour. The house was beautiful, just as I'd imagined it in my mind's eye. The house felt like a *stranger,* nonetheless. I sat at the bottom of the entry staircase, pulling my robe snug about my legs. Glory, Kris and Marv sat down beside me.

Kristen had been dating Marv for some time. He was a strikingly handsome young man with dark hair and penetrating blue eyes. Marv read the emotions I didn't realize were written graphically on my face. "Before long," he said, putting his hand on my knee, "memories will build up and it will start feeling like home."

∞∞∞

THANKSGIVING 1981. My mother, Velma, was still living in the old DeSoto home but spent weekends and special occasions with us. As each of our children got a driver's license, they'd take their turn picking up Mom and Jon. Shortly before Dad's death, Mom had begun showing signs of memory loss. She now had increasing dementia. A couple living in Mom's basement apartment watched out for her, grocery shopping and taking up one meal a day. Still, Dick and I agonized over how long Mother could manage alone—living in the home she loved, where familiar surroundings comforted her and memories of Dad filled the rooms.

Several years earlier, Dick's mother Eva, twice widowed, married a fine man named Elmer. She was a strong and independent woman,

Send Off

and a wonderful mother-in-law, never interfering. Eva was also an attentive, sweet grandmother.

Dick had only one sibling, an older sister, Betty, who lived in town. Betty was one of a kind, outgoing and talkative. For example, one day the phone rang at Betty's home. Her husband, Paul, heard her chatting for twenty minutes or so. "Who was that?" he asked. "Don't know. Wrong number," Betty had answered.

My mother, Scott and Glory, Betty and her family, Mom Eva and Elmer joined the rest of us for Thanksgiving dinner. Dishes were barely unpacked and here we were, starting to build a memory-bank and starting to wear off the newness of the house. The family crammed themselves into the bedroom where I was holed-up. We enjoyed a quick visit. Thanksgiving grace was offered before everyone seated themselves at the dining room table.

I was content just hearing their voices and laughter. Since it took a great deal more energy to sit up, I spent most of my time prone, even during mealtime. I'd developed an amazing talent: plate atop my chest, I could eat lying flat without choking to death. With my pillow plumped beneath my head and a towel beneath *two* plates, I lay savoring the wonderful meal. Turkey, of course, which Kris had started early in the morning, along with cranberries, potatoes and gravy, an extra large helping of stuffing (per my request), Betty's glazed sweet potatoes, and string beans with hollandaise sauce.

The other plate, resting further down on my stomach, held fresh fruit salad graced with pomegranates and whipping cream. On the

Send Off

side of the plate sat one of Eva's renowned homemade rolls. Later, I would have a moderate slice each of her pumpkin and lemon meringue pie—how could I not try both? Illness had done nothing to squelch my appetite. I thought back to my school days, when I was always ravenously hungry. I'd devour not only the whole of my lunch but friends' leftovers as well. Some things never change.

Jonny, who was now eleven, had been fed earlier and was in his room listening to his music box. I could hear the faint strains of *The Farmer in the Dell* amid my family's voices. Jonny would be holding the box against his ear, I knew. He always did.

We'd built a tiny corner niche for Jon between the kitchen and family room, large enough for a built-in bed with drawers beneath, and a wall of cupboards to hold his clothes and toys. The room had two narrow sliding doors opening on each side. With stretch gates across them, Jon could be 'with us' without watchful supervision. It was one-on-one, nowadays. Jonny was never mean spirited, just full-of-it, and was stronger than ever. Perhaps to tease, for attention or just out of boredom, Jon would often grab anything near. A plant, vase or chair could go a-flying.

My family. All here in our lovely new home. All except Dad. It still seemed unnatural not having my father with us. How often I felt his influence in my life.

Stuffed full now, I set the plates aside and looked out the window. It was a gorgeous day. The riotous colors of fall had softened into mauve, blue-grey, browns and amber. Trees had shaken their leaves,

Send Off

clutching the sky with naked fingers. The fall crispness seemed to bring form into minute focus—the sky backlighting the landscape with an electric blue.

How much I took for granted: citizenship in my beloved country, thanks to the sacrifice of myriads before me—bestowing the precious blessing of freedom. I'd never known deprivation. Never heard my children cry from hunger, or fear. Never listened in the dark of night for footsteps and a pounding on the door.

I had eyes to see and ears to hear, legs, arms and hands to move, hot water to fill the bathtub and heat and light to fill a room. I had in my life those I loved and those who loved me. Heaping abundance filled my life as heaping abundance had filled my dinner plate.

I focused on the faint buzzing of conversation coming from the dining room—the voices of my loved ones. I thought of the other voices that had influenced me through the years. Voice lessons—a rich melody lilting through the songs of my heart. Truly, today was a day filled with bountiful blessings. Surely it was a day of new beginnings for me. I would begin to heal. I knew it. My heart filled with a resurgence of great hope.

∞∞∞∞

The afternoon light faded to darkness early now. Snow sat on the ground. Weeks ago I'd said to our Sheltie, "Hang in 'til spring, sweet Millie. You'll feel better." We should have had her put to sleep.

Send Off

Minutes ago David told me he'd found her dead. He and Dick were burying her now, behind the barn.

I could see Millie as a pup, prancing about like a little princess. I could see her chasing after the kids; sitting proud and tall as David gave her a ride in the trailer behind the sit-down mower. I could see her lying on her spot by the door on Karren Street—always obedient, sweet and well-behaved. We called her our celestial dog. I let my heart mourn.

∞∞∞

Kristen knocked softly on my bedroom door, then peeked in. "Mom?"

"Hi, honey. So, how has your day gone?"

"Fine," she said, dropping onto the side of the bed where I'd been resting all day. Brushing a strand of hair aside, she cleared her throat and took a deep breath.

I peered at her more closely. My eighteen year old daughter's face was awash with anticipation. Something was up. Kris lowered her eyes, smoothed a patch of rumpled covers, looked to me and plunged in. "Mom, Marv and I want to get married."

I sucked in my breath. Not that the announcement came totally out of the blue. But so soon? My thoughts tumbled: *Oh, Kris. You're so very young. You need time to experience life—to stretch, to fly—before anchoring yourself to such a tremendous commitment. Marv is*

Send Off

wonderful . . . but . . .

"I know exactly what you're going to say, Mom." Scooting closer to me she hurried on. "Yes, I'm young. But you and Dad know I'm very mature for my age, all the responsibility I've had with your being sick, for one thing. I've thought it over for weeks. I've prayed about it. *We've* prayed about it. It's what I really want, Mom, and I'm ready." Kristen had one more comment. "I'll have one quarter of college finished by the time we're married." She stopped now, to let me speak. I spoke the words she knew I would.

∞∞∞

MARCH 18, 1982. I made it to the wedding ceremony, pushed in a wheelchair down the long corridors before hopping out to join the gathering. Dick's heart and mine had swelled to our throats as we held hands, watching our daughter being married.

Now, everyone was at the reception this snowy night. The house was quiet. *Turn Around . . .* The words of the old song played in my ears . . . *turn around . . . and you're grown, going out the door.* Cutting apron strings didn't get easier. Yet before long, Marv would feel like our son, just as Glory felt like our daughter. The wonderful thing about love is—it never runs out. There's always more to give.

Pitfalls

12

"What in the world is wrong, Jonny?" I gasped as Mark walked our thirteen year old son through the door. Jonathan hadn't been home for several weeks and I couldn't believe the change in him—thin as a skeleton. I noticed a tremor in his hand.

I grabbed the phone and called the school. I was informed Jonathan had been throwing up for weeks, causing the vomiting himself. He'd been sticking his finger down his throat, a behavior not uncommon with brain damaged children. Why was I not informed? Jon was obviously suffering from the effects of malnutrition. Immediately, I asked to be transferred to the physician on call.

A valve could be placed at the bottom of Jon's esophagus, keeping food from being regurgitated, I was told. I had Jonathan scheduled for surgery as soon as was possible.

This was not the best timing. Dick had just gone through minor knee and elbow surgery and was still limping. The day of the operation I watched the clock, longing to be at the hospital. Finally,

Pitfalls

Dick called, telling me the procedure had gone well. Jon was being wheeled into the ICU. Relief brought tears.

Now, I could laugh as I visualized the story Dick had related to me. In the hospital the night before, Dick with Scott and Glory, had spent time with Jon. Jon was hooked up to an IV and was restless. Receiving permission, the three of them took Jon for a walk down the lengthy hospital corridor.

Picture it: With Glory along side, Scott pushes the IV pole holding Jon under one arm, Dick, limping, holding him under the other. Jon sways on unsteady, toothpick legs which stick below the hospital gown. Down the dimly lit hallway a man approaches, carrying a tray of food.

Oh, my. Look at that. How sad, the man must have thought. *Poor little boy. Looks like he's on his last leg. And the man . . . his father? He's in pretty bad shape, too.* Closer they come. *Why in the world are they out walking him. The little kid looks so terribly weak and feeble.*

The gentleman proffers a sympathetic smile and steps aside for the foursome to pass. In split second timing, Jonny makes his signature flying-leap. Like a cannonball he shoots toward his target, grabbing the food tray then crashing with it to the floor. Like the woman at the zoo—sack of sandwiches snatched from her hand—the man's mouth gapes open. In repeated fashion, Jon begins snarfing up the food splattered on the floor. So much for feeble enervation.

I chuckled. Then sighed. *Oh, Jon. What are we going to do with you? Sticking your finger down your throat. You've picked some*

Pitfalls

doozies of behaviors. My thoughts burrowed through the years to the day when Jonny was nine years old. I'd received a particularly devastating phone call from one of the physicians at the Training School. I was informed that beside head-banging, Jonny had recently started another destructive behavior. He'd begun hitting and poking at his left eye. Perhaps headaches or eye pain had triggered the behavior, the doctor said. The doctor nonchalantly added, "Jonathan has caused an injury cataract and is now blind in that eye."

Blind? The word tore at my brain. Was he hitting his other eye? Was it at risk also? It was. What could be done to protect his sight? The doctor offered no suggestions.

I got in the car and drove down to troubleshoot the matter with Mike Snow, Self Help building supervisor. I was upset I'd not been told to begin with, but that was water under the bridge. At least I knew I'd find in Mike a caring, listening ear.

We discussed a number of possible solutions, but nothing viable until Mike mentioned shock therapy, which the school now prohibited using. It sounded archaic. Cruel. But would it work? I asked. "I think there's a good chance it would," Mike said.

"How bad would the shock be?"

"Uncomfortable but not really painful," Mike answered in his quiet voice.

"How would it work?"

Mike leaned back in his chair. "Well, we'd probably use an electrical prod. It's a wand about twelve inches long. We call it a

Pitfalls

zinger. Someone would monitor Jon during waking hours, and each time he hit or poked his eye he'd be given a mild shock," Mike explained. "Hopefully, Jon would associate discomfort with his behavior and stop. Theoretically it's very simple." Mike suggested I meet with the building psychologist, Kevin Morris, to discuss the subject. We'd need his input and support before further consideration.

I found Kevin a pleasant, capable person who, like Mike, cared deeply about the children. "What's your opinion?"

"It's no guarantee," he said, "but, yes, I think it would work. One thing you need to know, however," Kevin continued. "It's likely that if Jon quits bothering his eye, he'll simply adopt another behavior."

"Well . . . you know all the typical behaviors. Would any be as potentially threatening as going blind from hitting his other eye?" Kevin shook his head. "So . . . you recommend the therapy?"

Kevin took a deep breath. "Under the circumstances, yes. But I'll tell you, it will be an uphill battle getting permission."

I made an official request to Dr. Paul Sagers, the Training School's Superintendent. I was given a flat-out, *no*. Pumping up courage for several days, I called Dr. Sagers again. "Draw up a legal document absolving the school from all liability and I'll sign it," I importuned. "I feel this is the only course that might save Jon's sight."

Dr. Sagers relented and passed the issue to the Human Rights Committee for approval. Mike and Kevin pled the cause. Finally, we received consent and Kevin worked up a protocol for its

Pitfalls

implementation.

The procedure would be carefully monitored and meticulously documented. Kevin, himself, would operate the zinger the majority of time. With his expertise he believed only he could accurately evaluate Jon's responses and the program's safety. With the staff lending their support, even though it would mean extra work, we steeled ourselves and held our breaths. *Oh, Jonny. I'm sorry, sweetie. But, it's for your best good.*

With great dedication and generosity, Kevin Morris stayed by Jon's side—working ten-to-twelve-hour days, with little relief. The process took nearly a month, and to our joy it succeeded. Jonny quit hitting his eye.

In time, however, as Kevin predicted, Jon began another behavior. He started to lean his throat against an object, the side of a table, for instance, then press, choking himself. Providentially, it was felt Jon's choking was not cutting off his oxygen long enough to cause harm. Notwithstanding his prior optic nerve damage and poor eyesight, Jonathan could see out of one eye.

I pulled my thoughts to the present—to Jon's esophagus surgery—performed to keep him from throwing-up when he stuck his finger down his throat. *Oh, Jon. Couldn't you just bite your fingernails?*

*

The winter sun warmed the crust of snow. The sun's rays caught the myriad snow crystals, igniting them into blazing prisms. The

Pitfalls

night's frost—caked upon naked branches—had melted into shimmering drops and it seemed as if a thousand tiny lights were gracing field and tree, flashing in random pattern.

I filled my eyes with winter's dazzling show then glanced at the clock. Dick would be at the hospital with Jon a bit longer. He should be calling to let me know how Jonny was continuing with his recovery in the ICU.

Reviewing the past history of Jonny's challenges, my thoughts continued along the same track. Not long after the successful shock therapy, there was a decrease in federal and local funding at the school. Staffing was reduced and the quality of care likewise suffered. Jon's teacher Kathy Terry and I commiserated on the phone one day. What could be done?

Dick, Kathy and I reached a decision for Kathy to take-leave from the school and teach Jon herself. She rented a small, inexpensive apartment, where she taught him Monday through Friday during school hours. He returned to the Training School each evening and weekends. Rent, food and additional expenses were added to the salary we paid her. Dick and I felt the expense worth it if positive changes might increase the quality of Jon's future life.

Kathy implemented a specialized program developed for Jon by Robert Doman, Jr., founder of The National Academy for Child Development out of California. Bob Doman was a relative of Dr. Glen Doman whose Doman-Delcado patterning we'd followed years earlier.

Pitfalls

With a number of Utah clients, Doman came to Salt Lake quarterly for evaluations. We'd been given permission for Jon to remain a resident of the School while leaving campus six hours daily. The adventure began.

The apartment was decked out with olive green carpet and dark paneling. Intentionally, Kathy placed a few plants about, not only to brighten the dreary rooms, but to give Jonny opportunity to overcome his habit of grabbing. For the first several weeks Jon flew about the apartment, yanking out plants by their roots and flinging them across the room. He constantly tugged off his new eye glasses strapped on his head; opened the fridge and grabbed food; pushed over chairs; threw toys; massacred his lunch and choked himself on the kitchen table. Kathy buckled her seatbelt and hung on for dear life. In four months' time Jonathan's behavior was acceptable.

When Jon was little, he'd developed an endearing mannerism. He would squint his eyes and take a sidelong glance when looking at someone. Now, with his cataract, the trait became accentuated. While Kathy fixed lunch Jon sat still, small miracle in itself. He'd throw his squinty, sidelong look, letting her know he was thoroughly peeved at being kept waiting.

Jon was showing progress. His activities targeted cognizant development, object recognition, matching shape and colors and tactile development.

Jon loved his teacher. He'd run into Kathy's arms and as she lifted him for a hug, he'd cinch his legs around her waist. But Kathy was developing back trouble. "Oh, Jon, I'm sorry. I can't lift you anymore." she said, kneeling to give him a hug.

One morning, missing their routine, Jonny pushed a chair to where Kathy stood. He climbed atop, circled his arms around her neck and wrapped his legs about her waist, like a baby chimp clinging to its mother. "Jon, you're amazing," Kathy giggled, his display of thought-processing a delight to her.

A year passed. Jon was behaving and attending to his work, for the most part. His evaluations with Robert Doman indicated his level of achievement was improving. Still, it was an uphill battle. At the Training School—with an overworked staff—there was little reinforcement and follow-through to maintain Jon's good behavior. He'd simply revert to his old ways. How beneficial was Jon's tutoring, long-term? Should we discontinue? It was time for reassessment.

As it turned out, the decision was made *for* us. Lugging a massive carpet cleaning machine up a flight of stairs one day, Kathy injured her back. Jon returned to school full-time and Kathy spent extended time recuperating. We felt so bad about that. However, Kathy, Dick and I looked back on the year, viewing our enterprise a success. Jonathan had been given the opportunity to achieve maximum growth and we could take comfort that we'd tried to do our best by him. What gratitude I held for Kathy, who'd accomplished much, given much and loved much.

*

Pitfalls

The phone rang, bringing my thoughts to the present. Dick was calling from the hospital with an update on Jonny's recovery from the stomach surgery. Still in ICU, he was awake now, miserable, but doing as well as expected. With the valve in place, he would no longer be able to cause himself to regurgitate.

There had been other times of anxious waiting. When Jon was six years old we'd been told he had a brain tumor. A Cat scan was scheduled for the next week and tentative surgery, depending on test results. We should be prepared to lose him, the doctor said. Scott and Mark happened to be in their bedroom at the time we received the message. Dick and I called Kris and David in from play to join us there, and together we knelt alongside the bunk beds to offer a family prayer. We prayed for Jon's recovery, yet not wanting him to suffer or become more debilitated, we 'released' Jon to God—God's will be done. Tears were shed, but thankfully for naught. We'd sweat-out the week only to find the physician had misdiagnosed. What he thought to be a tumor was simply the optic nerve damage Jon had sustained at birth.

Years before, when Jon was two, he was operated on for a groin hernia. I sat in a tiny alcove off the hospital's long green hallway. Nine-forty. Ten-twenty. Ten twenty-nine. Finally, Jon's surgeon appeared. "Your son got along fine," he said. "While I had him opened up, I decided to remove his testicles," he added without missing a beat.

"*What?*" Surely I'd misunderstood! The man felt he was doing

Pitfalls

society a favor. At nearly three years of age, before the extent of Jon's brain damage became evident, Jon's potential seemed optimal. We'd worked so hard to help him function as normally as possible: We took him to Dr. Turkel in Detroit. We did Doman-Delacado patterning. *Then I'm told he's been sterilized?* It would take hours for me to come off the ceiling and consider the implications. Would the delicate hormonal balance in Jon's body be affected? I did not know. Certainly at puberty it would. What long-term effect would this surgery have on Jon's total well-being?

Dick and I would not sue, even though the outcome would be unequivocal. A drawn-out, traumatic medical review—stirring us up the more—would not bring back Jon's missing organs. We reported the doctor's horrendous conduct to the Utah State Medical Association and insisted the information be recorded on his medical record.

Life holds such moments. Moments of anxiety, injustice, trauma, sadness and challenge. We don't walk our path without them. Certainly, every parent faces moments of drama and challenge with each and every child.

But Dick and I would get through whatever Jon's future held. Surely Jon would recover from the esophagus operation and the current problem of malnutrition. Yet, in the years stretching ahead, was there a realistic hope of Jon making marked improvement behaviorally, mentally, or in his quality of life?

Oh, Jonny. What's going to happen to you? I wish you could

Pitfalls

clear out of this old world and not have to suffer longer. As terribly as I'd miss you, as horrendously hard as it would be, I want you to be free. I want you to be free, pumpkin—your bright, noble spirit unencumbered. Free to move on with your eternal progression.

Insights

Kathy Terry   *Totally Nerd*

The Training School

13

FEBRUARY 1983. Winter melted into spring. Outside my huge bedroom window—my portal to the outside world—as I lay in bed, I could see across the valley. To the west, the Oquirrh range hugged the horizon and to the south, Point of the Mountain jutted perpendicular to the Wasatch Range. There, with the unique air currents, hang-gliders gathered to soar the skies. Today, four or five circled above The Point. Through my binoculars I watched in fascination.

"Hi, Mom." It was Mark. He sauntered in and sat down on one of the overstuffed chairs. "How are you feeling?" he asked.

"Good, honey. How were classes today?"

Mark groaned. "I had two midterms."

"Oh, I didn't realize. How did you do?"

"I aced Western Civilizations. Hebrew, I don't know. It was brutal, but I think I did well."

A University of Utah student, he'd gone to Egypt on a dig at Tel El Shuqufiya where Egyptian and Greek ruins were being excavated.

Insights

It was dirty, hot, high adventure—plucking off college credits besides.

This was Mark's and my ritual, this enjoyable afternoon visit. It had been ours for years. "How's Syd?" I asked. Mark had begun dating coed Sydney, a diminutive and attractive blonde with a hint of freckles across her nose.

Months ago I'd asked, "So . . . is this getting serious?" "Naw. We're just good buddies," he had replied. *Sure,* I thought. Weeks later Mark announced his intention to marry. Sydney would join our family, once again giving us opportunity to open our arms and love another.

Only David would be home now. How could that be? It seemed such a short time ago our little family would pile into the station wagon and head for the cabin, with Millie panting in the back. Minutes ago, it seemed, we'd gone out to eat, pressed into a large booth with Jonny sitting nicely in a high chair beside us. Minutes ago, I'd help the kids with school projects spread across the kitchen table, there on Karren Street. Minutes ago the house was a hubbub of noisy activity, my children close about me, filling my busy days and filling my contented heart.

Days after Mark announced his marriage, I received a phone call from the Training School—calls often reporting some sort of problem. I was on the alert, but unprepared for the serious news. Jon had fallen and broken his jaw. The break would require a delicate operation securing a brace on the jawbone to keep the fracture stationary. Jon would need to be kept in arm restraints until the fracture healed.

Unfortunately, Dick was out of town, and I was not doing well. Mark rushed down, sweat-out the operation, sat by Jon's side in recovery and, missing classes, spent the next day. He stroked Jon's hands, arms and forehead, crooning comfort—and wept.

It turned out to be a five month nightmarish ordeal for Jon, as his jaw had great difficulty healing. Unable to be there to comfort and support my son, my tears came often. Jon spent long-term recovery in the small hospital unit at the School. To begin with, his wrists were tied to the bed railings. Cruel. Yet Jonny had to be kept from touching his jaw. Later, when I was able to visit, Jonny was wearing a jacket restraint with cardboard-tube sleeves—his arms unable to bend.

He managed to be cheerful those long months despite his frustrations and boredom. Jon's mettle melted my heart. Another bright spot in my heart was the upcoming wedding.

∞∞∞

JUNE 10, 1983. With Salt Lake experiencing a disastrous flood—sandbags lining the streets—I attended Mark and Syd's wedding ceremony and made the gala wedding breakfast as well. I was unable to attend the reception. The next morning, Mark and Syd

Insights

were off to Israel for a month's honeymoon, part of an excavation team at Tel Hemna in the Sorek Valley, where King Solomon met one of his wives. How many brides possessed such pluck?

∞∞∞

I felt strong enough to stay up later, like a grown-up. What a treat. Over the years, most early evenings, I'd had to head to bed (or remain in bed), shut away while Dick also spent the night alone. I was stretched out on our navy blue couch in the family room, with Dick in an easy chair reading the paper. Soon, *Magnum P.I.* would be starting on TV and I'd catch another episode. The house was quiet. (When David was around—usually with a handful of friends—the house rocked.) With *Magnum* coming on to distract me, my thoughts would not circle-around to health issues. Many questions remained.

Over the years, I *had* discovered valid elements of my mystery illness. Recently, a doctor had been recommended to me. Hoping my new physician might act as a detective, piecing together the clues of my myriad symptoms to form a solid diagnosis, I began my story—carefully citing my long list of symptoms. Had I found a doctor who would take me seriously? A Sherlock Holmes MD who would be committed and dogged in his investigation?

My effort lay in presenting precious evidence, not *reveling* in the narrative. As I listed my symptoms, the doctor's eyes glazed over. Once again I knew I was being labeled a neurotic—I recognized the

Insights

look. Not that I could blame him. I sounded like one.

Surely, new knowledge about my strange illness was emerging somewhere. Surely, someone 'out there' knew something. Yet the door I'd just opened so hopefully clanged shut, simultaneously with the doctor's open-mindedness.

Dutifully, I continued my yearly physical exams. I kept seeking assistance for my malady from mainstream medicine. Still, diagnostic testing revealed nothing definitive. What tremendous respect I had for the medical profession; for the integrity and dedication of marvelous physicians and scientists whose expertise I so greatly needed. I would keep trying.

Nonetheless, when portals close or lead to dead ends, one usually becomes ever so open-minded, ever so ready to open a new door, to peek in and to evaluate. Truth lies in varied corridors, not just one. I opened the doors available to me, focusing on alternative medicine.

∞∞∞∞

Apprehension knotted my stomach. In all honesty, I didn't want someone poking around in my head. Dr. Alan Beardall, DC,[10] practicing in Portland, Oregon, had just made a provocative statement. "I sense you have an emotional problem with perfectionism, and it's affecting your physical health." *Who, me? Perfect little me having an emotional problem? Well . . . sure, I'm a bit hard on myself. But an emotional problem?* He continued, "I send some of my patients to a psychologist named Mike Gottesman for counseling. He's extremely effective, especially with this particular issue. Would you like an appointment?" Who knew what might be lurking around in some little corner of my mind? For several seconds I felt terribly vulnerable.

I swallowed down my anxiety, surprised it was there. After all, I'd been taking a look at my feelings for several years now. I'd been to the psychiatrist once—about Jon. "Sure," I answered. "Make an appointment."

I was in Oregon for a week of treatments from Dr. Beardall, and now on my way to see psychologist Mike Gottesman. I found Gottesman a pleasant young man, kind and intuitive. After a brief chat, getting a feel for my background, he said, "I'm going to use something called hypnotherapy. It's different than hypnosis, for you'll remain fully awake. After achieving a state of relaxation, I'll guide your mind back in time to issues you've forgotten consciously but which are stored in your brain.

"All right," he continued. "Get comfy. Close your eyes, breathe deeply, and let's find out when you first felt such pressure to be perfect.

"You're going deeper . . . deeper . . . deeper into relaxation. Your mind and body are fully relaxed," he intoned. "Now Sondra, I want you to go back in time . . . back through the years . . . back . . . back to the first time you felt compelled to be perfect. Back . . . How old are

Insights

you?"

"Seven," I replied, surprised, not knowing if seven was the correct answer. It simply 'felt' right.

"Good. I want you to picture yourself at seven. In your mind's eye, see your seven-year-old self sitting beside you." I did so. "Now, take your little child-self into your arms. Tell her she's wonderful just the way she is."

As I imaged holding my little self and talking to her, I was suddenly overwhelmed with emotion. My heart welled full of exquisite love for this little self. I understood some of what she was feeling. Stored in her little heart was a great anxiety. A terrible need to be good. Other feelings pulsed there, ones I couldn't quite identify. Shame? Guilt?

My heart flooded with compassion. I was unable to hold back sobs. "Let your emotions come," Mike said. Self-consciously I sobbed on. After a while he continued, "Comfort her. Let her know she's perfectly wonderful just the way she is. She doesn't have to try harder or be better."

Mike coached me along until we sensed my child-self had released her troubled feelings, and had been consoled. The experience astounded me. *I had tapped into feelings I'd had as a child.* I couldn't imagine what circumstance had caused them. What amazed me most, however, was feeling such incredible tenderness, compassion and empathy; feeling such perfect, pure love for myself.

Insights

My mind flew back to the day I'd taken a walk under the huge maple trees on Karren Street—when Jonny was tiny; when my heart had been touched by the spirit, flooding with love and gratitude—with love for all of God's creations. I thought of the profound love I'd felt for the woman and child—strangers I'd met on the street. I realized I was now experiencing that same deep quality of love for my little child-self. I knew by comparison, that never before had I *truly* felt pure, unconditional charity for myself.

In those moments, I saw not only how precious I was as a child, but how precious I was now—in spite of my weakness and foibles, in spite of my inadequacies and blemishes. Isn't it often easier for us to love others than to love ourselves? Yet, before we can express love with full charity—with patience, kindness, mercy, compassion and forgiveness—before we can glimpse the magnificence of the soul, isn't one important key to first love ourselves? I still struggle to practice this lesson.

I am not talking about egotism, self-centeredness or vanity. Don't we often feel guilty or even foolish when giving ourselves deserved commendation? Perhaps, we feel it prideful to acknowledge a job well done, to delight in our particular blend of qualities, talents and gifts. We feel it unseemly to believe we're simply grand despite our weaknesses.

My job is to see myself as God sees me, and to remember I am precious simply because I exist; to understand I am unique. I have a

Insights

purpose in life. I can accomplish—I can touch lives in a way no other person can—because of my individual uniqueness and purpose, despite what I am lacking.

"So what can I be? What can [you] be? We can be what [God] designed us and intend[s] us and help[s] us to be. How does one fill the measure of his or her creation? [We do so] by thrusting in a sickle and reaping with all our strength—and by rejoicing in our uniqueness and our difference. To be all that you can be, your only assignment is (1) to cherish your course and savor your own distinctiveness, (2) to shut out conflicting voices and listen to the voice within, which is God telling you who you are and what you will be, and (3) to free yourself from the love of profession, position, or the approval of men by remembering that what God *really* wants us to be is someone's sister, someone's brother, and someone's friend."[11] Even our own friend.

∞∞∞

I circled the back lawn, my steps fairly brisk, yet careful not to overextend myself. A far cry from jogging, but it was a start. *Again.* I needed some sort of mild exercise. I plopped down onto a lounge chair to rest, gazing at the mountains leaning against the sky. How wonderful to be feeling stronger. Were things *finally* falling into place?

Insights

I had continued taking great care to protect myself against chemical exposures, molds and mildew; monitored my hypoglycemia and food allergies; eaten wholesomely; continued my relaxation, affirmation and visualization techniques—and recently I'd had my alloy (silver) fillings removed. Although, in general, amalgam fillings were thought to be benign, there was a growing concern among certain health practitioners that mercury in silver fillings leached out into the body, wreaking havoc with sensitive individuals.

Lead, mercury, etc., are difficult to detoxify naturally and usually end up being stored in bodily tissue, poisoning and/or suppressing the immune system. When I'd worked as a dental assistant years ago, after mixing the amalgam, the excess mercury was expelled by hand and the alloy mixture squeezed into a cotton pad. Unaware, I'd absorbed mercury through my skin. When I was two years old, I'd tasted a spoonful of white paint thinking it looked like a vanilla malt. It was filled with lead. So, here I was being treated for toxic metal poisoning.

My adrenals had been an issue from the beginning of my illness, I believed—being jammed into overdrive to a state of complete exhaustion. I was on specific nutritional support for them, and also for hormonal support.

Best of all, Dr. Beardall's treatments seemed significantly helpful. Now, aware of my need to watch for 'perfectionism' sticking up its head, I was certainly attacking my illness from a variety of directions.

Insights

What was or was not working I wasn't sure, but wonderfully, I was doing better.

Missing Us

14

SEPTEMBER 1984. Mom had been in a retirement center for a time—a room with her own furniture, paintings and familiar treasures. I called every day and looked forward to her spending each weekend with us.

I would help Mom with a shower and shampoo. At my vanity, I'd put up her hair with bright pink rollers, pluck her eyebrows and catch other stray hairs. "So old . . . I look so old," she'd sigh. After a comb-out and makeup I could truthfully say, "Oh, Mom, look how beautiful you are." She had a full head of white hair, not thin and yellowed like many her age. Her eyes were still lovely. Yet, I could see a veil of fear and confusion in her eyes as her dementia deepened, as she searched for words, searched for a memory.

Finished at the vanity, I would kiss her on the cheek and help her up, hiding my sorrow. I would crawl back to bed, utterly exhausted from the small but welcomed effort. Once again, after significant improvement in my health—despite all the endeavors—I was on a downward spiral. Caught in the vortex, Dick struggled to keep his grasp, to hang onto a vestige of hope.

Several years earlier, Dick and his business partner sold their employee benefit and administrative firm to a national company. Dick became president of the benefits division and senior vice president in the company. He found the role and his traveling schedule to New York increasingly demanding, and was considering an early retirement. The matter weighted heavily on him.

I weighed heavily. I felt like a millstone around his neck. Was I *ever* going to get well? How long would he continue being saddled with me? This thin, bedraggled woman spending her life in bed. He needed a vivacious, lovely wife, dressed up, smelling of perfume and going places with him. Here I lay in some ratty old nightgown year after year.

Dick hungered, longed, for a normal life, for a normal, fulfilling companionship. I felt tremendously guilty, unable to be the wife he needed and wanted. I loved Dick enough to let him go. Yet he'd stand by me, I knew. So why was I even thinking this way?

Dick's way of dealing with the stress of my illness was to distance himself from it. From me. I began feeling like an inanimate object, lying in my room month after month through each passing year, isolated and barely keeping my nose above water. Yes. I was heavy as a millstone, near drowning us both.

In a figurative sense, I had to lay the mantle of my stewardship as a mother and as a homemaker upon Dick. Surely, he somehow sensed this imperceptible burden, in addition to everything else he carried. I could see stress taking its toll on my dear husband. He exhibited headaches and fatigue and had to start blood pressure medication. We were both drained dry, physically, mentally and emotionally.

My weakness was so profoundly deep it took all I had to hold on a day at a time. I'd conserve hours of energy just to visit a few minutes with a measure of animation. I tried masking the depth of my struggles. What purpose would it serve to lay bare the whole of it? I was doing all I could medically and emotionally. I was simply trying to cope, trying to choose hope over despair; gratitude over complaint; peace over fear. If my loved ones were filled with additional anxiety and discouragement, it would be harder to manage my choices.

Weeks earlier, Mother had a doctor's appointment. She was diagnosed with the beginning of congestive heart failure. She could live for years, or go any time. The phone rang. It was Mom. "I'm…I…my heart. I think I'm dying."

I talked to Mother, calming her. Although I'd received similar calls, they were always extremely unnerving. I'd notify the front desk and have someone check in, I told her. We'd bring her to our house for a few days until she felt better.

Mom experienced occasional arrhythmia and periods of faintness. Of course she felt frightened and vulnerable. So did I. She needed to live with us. She needed me to take full-time care of her. *I wanted to, with all my heart.* Always before, I'd flowed along with the little nitty-gritties and the heart-stoppers that are a part of life. But I'd

Missing Us

begun feeling tremendous pressure about Mom. I was ready to shatter—like glass.

It was time to be accountable to myself, to Dick and to my family. To Mother. I had to gather courage to tell my siblings one of them needed to take over her care. Weeks later, I finally picked up the phone to make arrangements.

Mother would be going to South Dakota to live with my oldest brother Jay, his wife Marilyn and their three children. Jay and Marilyn were professors at South Dakota State University. Marilyn, as a daughter-in-law, would shoulder a tremendous weight, and I felt profoundly grateful to them both for assuming mother's care.

Dick and David would drive Mother to the airport after I said good-bye. *Oh Mom. Will I ever see you again? Dear, dear, dearest Mother.* Memories tumbled in throughout the night.

∞∞∞

LOS ANGELES, CALIFORNIA—1944

I was late for class. My siblings had lit out for school long ago. "I'll have to give you a ride," Mom said, exasperated with my dilly-dallying. Dad had the family car at work. Mom wheeled my brother Jay's bike out of the garage, the only bike in the family.

I stole a glance at Mom. So rarely was she perturbed that I felt apprehensive, but she looked as kindly and serene

Missing Us

as ever.

My mother's oval face was set with high cheek bones and exquisite, large blue eyes—topped with thick, somewhat unruly brows. She had a lovely, shy smile which revealed an ever-so-thin strip of gold inlay along the bottom of one front tooth. Hers was rather an ordinary yet expressive face, but I thought it the most beautiful in the world. On close observation, Mom's dark hair was showing strands of grey. She had remained slender, from running up and down the stairs of our multilevel home.

Mother swung one leg over Jay's bike, straddling, her housedress hiked above her shapely legs. She hoisted me sideways onto the bar. "Hang on," she cried, pushing off. I'd never seen Mom ride. I didn't even know if she could. "Keep your feet away from the spokes," Mom called as she pumped up Panorama Terrace.

I'd never been taken on a ride. I gripped the handlebars, desperately trying to find my balance. Mom turned down onto Silverlee, so steep it seemed perpendicular. Holy cow. My eyes bugged. My stomach flip-flopped. My mouth went dry.

Mom expertly braked her way down the treacherous curve as, white knuckled, I held on for dear life. She flew

Missing Us

the rest of the way down Silverlee, jogged onto Silverado and in a moment's time turned us onto Griffith Park Boulevard, straight sailing here on out. Finally I inhaled and loosened my grip. Why, Mom was absolutely stupendous.

Her expertise shouldn't have surprised me. Mom could do about anything. My Mother, Velma Andelin, was born in Utah in 1900—truly a twentieth century woman. She was the first female yearbook editor and cheerleader in her high school. Mom wrote her first play as a senior. The drama teacher felt that it was so good that she asked Mom to produce it.

After graduation, with three other adventurous spirits, Mom took a *five hundred* mile hike through a mountain wilderness. Then, receiving her teaching certificate at the University of Utah, she taught in the wilds of Wyoming—in Star Valley—in a little school with a potbelly stove.[12] Later, joining her family that had moved to California, Mother taught art in junior high school and to adult night classes. While teaching, she met Dad on a blind date.

Through the years Mother wrote a number of three-act plays and various productions for church and community gatherings. She was set and costume designer, makeup artist, sound effects and prompter, all in one. Her productions

Missing Us

WERE ALWAYS PROFESSIONAL.

MOTHER TAUGHT ME TO APPRECIATE BEAUTY. MOTHER TAUGHT ME TO SEEK THE GOOD. MOTHER TAUGHT ME I COULD DO ANYTHING TO WHICH I SET MY MIND.

VOICE LESSONS. MOTHER'S GREATEST GIFT WAS THAT SHE LOVED ME, HER LEGACY A RICH MELODY LILTING THROUGH THE SONG OF MY HEART.

∞∞∞

It's time for Mom to leave for the airport, to fly to South Dakota. Dick and David help Mother into the car. I stand at the door, waving good-bye. I blow her a kiss, like the ones she used to blow to me. They drive off and I walk back to bed.

The years vanish and I find myself home again in California, on Panorama Terrace. Mental snapshots slide into place: I perch on the corner of the kitchen bench, watching mother cook. She smiles at me; I help on wash day, turning the wringers above the machine while Mom feeds through the clothes—into the sink of rinse water they plop; Mother kneels at her bedside in prayer. She doesn't know I've come to the door. I can't hear her words. I know God does.

Mother is holding my babies, petting Millie, kissing Dad. I see love in Mom's eyes. Always. Forever. But now I see the fear and disorientation, too. The look haunts me. *Oh, Mama. I wanted to keep taking care of you. I didn't want you to have to leave.* Sobs start deep in my viscera, working their way up. I cry them dry.

∞∞∞

I waited a few days to call after Mom's arrival in Dakota, letting her settle in. "I don't . . . I want . . . home. To come home. To take care of you," Mother said, remembering I was ill. She just needed more time, I thought, brushing away my tears. My next call agitated her more. Mother cried, pleading I come and get her. I'd wait a while to phone. I'd write instead. Even my letters upset her. Jay and Marilyn were keeping me posted.

After several weeks Mom was still asking to "go home," but seemed to be making some adjustments. She was loved and being sweetly cared for I knew, which comforted me.

One last time I spoke with Mother. My call blew apart all progress. I could not put her through this again—put Jay, Marilyn and myself through this again. Letters would even have to be postponed. Contrary to every feeling within my heart, *I had to exercise sufficient love to let Mom forget me.*

∞∞∞

For hours I had been lying still as a corpse, my eyes closed to the October sun—slanting its rays of the light through my window. My mind had not been still, however. *I'm a millstone.* I had said this to myself weeks earlier. Attaching a label to my emotions had been enlightening, but I had not pursued the issue. Today, I took my light of awareness into some deep, murky recess and thrust its beam upon the shadows. There, a mass of feelings lay tangled beneath the millstone. I crow-barred the stone aside and hacked off the ties that bound me to it, then I came up for air. How could I have been listening to my *voices*—moving forward in awareness—and missed recognizing that massive stone?

I filled my lungs with the emancipating, healing air, free now. No longer would I *allow* myself to feel guilt and responsibility for making Dick's life 'miserable.' I already knew each person alone is responsible for the way he or she reacts to life's challenges. I just hadn't applied the principle to this aspect of our lives.

Of course I felt bad that my illness was such a stress on us. *Of course* I felt compassion and sorrow for all the additional challenges, responsibilities and limitations my illness put on my dear husband. However, I now chose to perceive our adversity as a precious gift. From it, Dick was also having an opportunity for growth and the refinement of his soul. Ultimately, it was his choice and responsibility as to how he perceived and reacted to this trial. Casting aside my guilt removed a crushing burden from my soul.

Dick was at the other end of the house. "Come here when you can, honey," I called over the intercom. I was lying on my side of our king-sized bed. The other side had been empty for several years. I'd always been a light sleeper, but with my illness came terrible insomnia. Finally, we'd been forced to sleep in separate bedrooms.

Missing Us

Another isolation for us both.

"Need something?" Dick poked in his head.

"Yes. *You*. Come here," I said. "Take five."

Dick stretched out on top of the bed, plumping a throw pillow under his head. I reached for his hand and twined my fingers through his. "I've been lying here thinking about you. How you're my sweetheart and very best friend," I said, pulling our hands to my lips and kissing his fingers. "I've been thinking how terrific you are, and that I'm so sorry for all the burdens you carry. I just wanted to tell you how much I appreciate all you do for me." I lifted our intertwined fingers to my cheek, resting them there. "All the years of grocery shopping you've done, for instance," I continued. "I know how much you hate that." Dick let out a groan. "And doing the cooking, dishes and the wash, all the times when I can't."

"I don't mind washing clothes," he said.

"Really?" I answered, surprised. I knew what else he disliked. "Well then, your having to wait on me, running my errands and my unending list of honey-do's." Dick groaned again. We laughed. "But most of all I appreciate your support. You never grumble about all the medical expenses. Everything I want to try you go along with. You're always there for me." I leaned my face to his and kissed his cheek. "Do you know how much that means?" I asked. "I could never get through all of this without you. Anyway, I haven't said thank-you for a while."

Dick turned to me and stroked my hair. He let out a deep breath.

"I'm sorry when I don't handle things very well. When I lose my cool. When I pull away. I just get so frustrated and so darn discouraged."

"You do great. Think about it, Honey. How many husbands would have stuck it out under the same circumstances?"

"Not many, I guess. It's . . . well, it's just that I miss *you*. I'm so tired of going places alone. It's such a lousy deal. Well, not as lousy as your having to lie here all the time," he added, "but I miss *us,* our being together, our going out . . . our holding hands in the car." With his face still turned to me, I watched a tear seep out the corner of his eye then roll along the side of his nose. Roughly, Dick wiped it away. I was glad he could cry—this man of mine. Swallowing down the pain Dick continued, "I miss waking up in the morning with you beside me. I get so lonely I don't know what to do with myself."

"Me too." I let out a long sigh. "But we'll keep hanging in. Somehow we're going to make it." I snuggled my head onto his shoulder.

"I love you," he said. "I know," I replied.

Bus Ride

15

SEPTEMBER, 1984. I was at my first appointment with psychiatrist, Dr. Frank Garner, MD—age, late thirties, I guessed, with dark hair and horned-rimmed glasses. Dr. Garner filled the room with a kindly, non-judgmental openness. Immediately, I felt comfortable. We spent the first session discussing my background and intent. I was there because Dr. Garner used a holistic approach in therapy and I wanted to become more effective in using visualization and meditation—techniques he encouraged.

"All right, I think I have a handle on you," he said with a genial smile. "See how this fits. You're extremely sensitive in nature. You're also extremely intuitive. You pick up on people's feelings loud and clear. Things affect you deeply, from soup to peanuts. How am I doing?" We laughed.

"Your extreme sensitivity is a wonderful gift, Sondra. It makes you empathetic and allows beauty to profoundly touch and nourish you. You probably cry hearing beautiful music or when you watch a

Bus Ride

sunset, right?"

"Boy, do you have me nailed."

"But your sensitivity has a flip side, as you're well aware. You wish you had a thicker skin. We'll work on it, on your perfectionism. But for the next few sessions, I'll take you on some meditations. Show you some visualization techniques that should be helpful to draw-in healing energies."

Several days later, on a lovely Indian summer morning, I lounged on our terrace, the sun friendly and warm on my face. In the stillness I could hear the faint crowing of a rooster. A butterfly lit nearby, fanning its wings. I closed my eyes, floating into relaxation. A perfect time to do some inner work.

Since my session with Mike Gottesman in Oregon, nearly a year earlier—when I connected with my child-self—I'd been using Gottesman's technique to unearth issues from my past. I felt I'd experienced valid insights and released a number of negative emotions.

Taking a deep breath, I instructed my mind: *Go back. To some specific issue that needs addressing. One that is adversely affecting me. I am willing to acknowledge it. To release it. Go back.* I continued deep breathing, stilling my mind.

Okay, I said to myself. How old am I? Seven, came the thought. Then, rather than impressions or feelings, as had always come before, into my mind flashed a scene, vivid and clear, as if unfolding on a movie screen:

Bus Ride

I have a dime in my shoe. I don't have money often. I've felt the pressure of the coin all through school—whispering possibilities. Today, Mom braided my hair. I wear a pinafore and huaraches. The dime stays put, down by my toes. It won't slip out the open heel, I know.

Sometimes I walk home with my brother, Gary, or with friends who go part way in my direction. Today I'm by myself. Kitty-corner from school sits a little shop. I walk in, across the white octagon-tiled floor with a crack down the middle. Overhead, a ceiling fan twirls shadows on the wall. The shop is fragrant with the smell of cigars. 'Hand-rolled from Havana' the sign says.

I pass the magazine racks then browse the display of playing cards. I look longingly at several decks, especially the one with the Persian cat sitting so proud and snobby. I have a card collection, and it's a good one.

But I've come to check out the candy. I brush my braids behind my shoulders and peer in the glass counter. It's stocked with Baby Ruths, Aba Zabas, Nicolettes, waxy red lips and sets of white buckteeth that taste like peppermint. There's Blackjack gum and suckers. I am tempted. I might walk further on, though, to the grocery store. Get myself half an apple-turnover at the bakery—

Bus Ride

ten cents worth.

No . . . I think I'd rather treat myself to a ride. I'll walk straight along Sunset Boulevard to the junction, where Santa Monica and Hollywood Boulevard begins. I'll catch the Hyperion bus that takes a big loop. I'll ride around once, then part way again, getting off near home. It's a wonderful ride.

I walk down the street. I'm nearly there. I glance into a store window, enthralled with the display. But I can't dillydally. If I'm home in pretty good time, Mom won't worry. I know not to talk to strangers. Never to get in someone's car. There are bad people around. But I've never seen any. I feel safe in my wonderful neighborhood. I'd better run. The bus sits on the corner, doors open. If I miss it I'll have to walk on home.

There, now, I pull my bare foot from my huarache and grab my dime, warm and sweaty. I drop the dime into the coin box. The box makes a whirling, clicking noise like it's counting the change. I walk to the middle of the bus and sit on the left, on a green leather seat. The bus is nearly empty. A nice lady sits up front, wearing hat and gloves. A couple sit in back.

The bus will drive down Hyperion, then swing past

Bus Ride

John Marshall High School. My brother, Jay and sister Vel Dean go there. I love Marshall High. It's so beautiful—it's red brick with fancy stonework around the front entry. We'll pass over the Franklin Bridge. There's no water under, just a street. It's beautiful, too. The bridge.

A man steps aboard. He's wearing an old black suit. It's wrinkled and dirty. He has a hat on. He looks at me and smiles, his teeth streaked yellow. One missing. I smile back, thinking I should be friendly. The man sits across the aisle from me.

With a loud hiss, the doors close, and we're off. I snuggle in for the ride, gazing out the window. My nose itches. If I wanted, I could scratch it without hands. I learned a trick once. Turn my head side to side—real fast—and my braids fly up and flip my face.

The man makes a funny cough. I look over. He smiles, then nods, looking down at his pants. He unzips them and pulls something out. I have never seen a man's private parts. He wiggles it, smiling at me again. This is something terribly wrong. Terribly bad. I hurry and look away. Out the window. The sun is shining just so, making a reflection. I see the man again, in the reflection, still

Bus Ride

GRINNING, STILL WIGGLING IT.

THE REFLECTION BRINGS GREATER HORROR TO ME. I CLOSE MY EYES. I TURN MY HEAD AWAY. I KNOW HE'S STILL LOOKING AT ME. HIS EYES POKE ME LIKE STICKS. MY FACE TINGLES HOT. MY HANDS ARE CLAMMY. I'M SICK TO MY STOMACH. I WANT TO RUN AWAY. RUN TO THE LADY. RUN TO THE DRIVER. BUT I'M GLUED TO THE SEAT. I'M SO VERY, VERY AFRAID.

A VOICE SPEAKS INTO MY MIND. *YOU'RE A BAD, BAD GIRL. YOU LOOKED*, IT SAYS. *THAT WAS AN AWFUL THING TO DO. NOW DADDY AND HEAVENLY FATHER WON'T LOVE YOU ANYMORE.* I HEAR THE VOICE LOUD IN MY BRAIN. IT CONTINUES. *BUT MAYBE, JUST MAYBE*, IT SAYS, *IF YOU NEVER, EVER, EVER DO ANYTHING WRONG AGAIN IN YOUR WHOLE LIFE—MAYBE THEY WILL FORGIVE YOU. IF YOU'RE PERFECT FROM NOW ON.*

The scene in my mind cut off as if a plug were pulled from a movie projector. The voice still reverberated, loud and accusing. I opened my eyes, taking a huge breath. My heart was pounding. I took another breath and gathered my composure. I'd never remembered the event. I must have blanked it out. Yet I knew it was true. With every fiber of my body I knew.

What amazed me most was hearing the thoughts that came from some part of my subconscious mind. They'd been recorded and stored in my brain. Like one of those old, cracked records we'd discovered at Lake Arrowhead when we found the Victrola record player, the accusation and the demands must have been playing over and over throughout the years. No *wonder* I had a problem with perfectionism.

Certainly, the exposure was a far cry from sexual molestation. Nonetheless, the event held profound consequences for me. Understand that in my generation, typically, sexual issues were never discussed. Sex was not placed graphically before children's eyes as it is now. I was an innocent. Suddenly, a measure of my 'purity' and 'innocence' was shattered, my sanctity violated. As is the normal pattern for a child, I took responsibility and blame. I held the shame and guilt.

I had placed, unknowingly, an impossible edict on myself; a yardstick for constant judgment and censure. Obviously, it had taken its toll, this tremendous subconscious burden—this 'trying to be perfect.' Now I keenly understood the relationship between my perfectionism and my illness.

I lay there on the terrace at the base of the mountains, marveling. *I'd actually tapped into a specific, traumatic event.* I was astounded. But seven years old? That couldn't be right. Too young. I wouldn't have been skirting around, so little.

Wait a minute. Seven? *Seven.* Probably close to eight and in second grade. So, it was true. "Go back," Gottesman had said. "Back in memory to the first time you felt such a need to be perfect. How old were you?" "*Seven*," I'd answered. This scene was what I'd opened-up in Oregon, when such overwhelming emotion spilled out. It all fit. This event was the initial trigger-point starting my desperate need to be 'perfect'.

I was tremendously excited. I could release the whole issue. Layers. Implications. Surely, releasing this event would facilitate excellent progress in my getting well.

∞∞∞

"Wonderful work, Sondra," Dr. Garner said. "Normally, I'd need to help you release the negative emotions stored from that experience, but it's my sense that you completed the process with Gottesman. Now, this will sound strange. I want you to create a safe, special place for your little child-self to live. You see," he continued, brushing a piece of lint from his slacks, "the child-self within *all* of us exists as rather a separate entity. An energy influencing and coloring much of our adult life.

"Your *child* needs to know she's absolutely safe, existing in a place where no harm will ever come, where she can be free and happy. Just talk to her about where she'd like to be. She'll tell you," he finished, patting my leg. "I'll be back in a few minutes."

Seriously? Well. . . "Okay," I said, hoping I could do it. I took a deep breath and relaxed. I visualized myself at seven—as if I were sitting beside myself. "Hi," I said. I sensed myself much younger. About three. Okay, I thought. I guess I'm supposed to work with my younger child-self.

In my mind's eye, I sat beside her and gave her a hug. "I love

Bus Ride

you," I said. "You're so wonderful, so good. Now, you're always going to live in a place where you're safe and happy, okay? Where no one can harm you." I imagined kissing her forehead and stroking her hair.

Was this working? I thought it was, for I was beginning to feel a welling-up of strong love, of deep tenderness and delight for this little self. In poured greater emotion, like I'd experienced in Oregon. I reached up and wiped a tear from my eye. "Okay, little Sonie. Where would you like to live? At home, or someplace else?"

An impression came, a feeling. Even though I still wondered if the process was succeeding, and still felt a bit foolish despite the love that had come flooding in, I let the impression take *word*. "No. I want to see Mommy and Daddy when I want to, but I want to live in a magical forest," I perceived her saying. "And have a unicorn as a friend . . . and a lion. And I want Jesus to come and visit me all the time. And I want to be able to fly."

"Okay," I said. "You can go there now. You'll always be safe and happy."

I'd heard no voice, as it were, like the 'voice' playing in my mind when I sat on our terrace and relived the bus experience. Yet somehow this impression seemed clear and precise. I couldn't *begin* to glimpse the complexity of the human psyche, how all this stuff worked. It seemed surreal. But I'd experienced truth, I believed, at Gottesman's, on the terrace and here, too. This was fascinating.

"Finished?" Dr. Garner asked, poking in his head.

Bus Ride

"Yep." I told him my child's wishes. We chuckled.

"Great. I want you to periodically check-in with her. Ask her how she's doing." Dr. Garner helped upright the reclining chair. "Keep up the good work, Sondra." My heart filled with gratitude for this wise teacher who'd come into my life and for all the other care-givers who had helped and supported me.

Joy and Pain

16

1988. Jonny lays his head on my shoulder. "That's nice, Jon," I say. We sit on a quilt under a huge sugar maple tree, branches thick with leaves. A movement of air flickers shadows on us as the overhead sun seeps through. We are out behind Jon's classroom at the Developmental Center, as the school is now called. Dick is taking a walk. I am pleased it's a good health-day for me to visit.

Jonny steals his sidelong glance at me, then giggles. I study his face, take it in my hands and kiss his forehead. "Oh, Jonny, you're looking so trashed now, aren't you, pumpkin?" I say, not bothered. That's the way it is.

Jonny rolls away but sits quietly, lifting his eyes to me. The cataract fills half his pupil—chalk white. I reach to pat his leg then stroke his arm. "Come closer and I'll scratch your back," I offer, but he stays put.

Jon's face looks lopsided. Maybe only I notice. His tongue lolls out between missing teeth, as if oversized for his mouth. I see his

Joy and Pain

scars, knowing most of their stories.

"You're being so good. How come you're so mild today?" I ask. I lie down to rest, alert. Jonny could suddenly lunge at me; he doesn't know his strength. Usually he grabs at my arms, pinching, bruises a testament of his interaction. "I'm so glad I felt strong enough to come with Daddy to visit, Jon. I get so lonesome when I don't see you."

Jonny puts his hand to his mouth, letting out the old familiar war-whoop. He giggles again. "What's so funny?" I ask. "Mama loves your laugh. Did you know how much I love your laugh?" My heart stretches with joy for my little son. He's eighteen, looking ten or eleven. *People think since you're 'retarded'*—I continue my conversation non-verbally—*that you're unaware, that things don't matter.*

Life is hard, isn't it, sweetheart? You get so terribly bored. You get frustrated. Oh, how you must long to communicate. To tell someone you're thirsty. Or your shoe pinches. Or you have a stomachache. You want to do things. Feel greater meaning. Feel some sort of accomplishment. I wish you could play touch football. Read a little story. Anything. You understand enough to feel 'lack.' I know you do. Yet you're always so patient. So good natured.

"Did you know that's what I especially love and admire about you, Jon?" I say out loud. "That you find things to be happy about. You make choices, even with your limited capacities. I'm proud of you, Jon."

Loud, guttural noises burst into my ears, then mellower sounds.

Joy and Pain

Jonathan laughs again, his face lit with the stretch of a smile. He continues the giggles, his thin little shoulders hitching up and down in rhythm. "What's tickling your funny bone, huh?" I ask, grinning back. I think he's simply happy to have me near.

Jonny giggles anew. "*What?* Are you thinking about something funny? Well, I am. Remember the time Kristen walked you onto the diving board and jumped with you into the pool? You were so terrified, you nearly strangled her, clutching on so tight. Thinking it over, you started laughing your head off. Remember?"

We were silent for a time. "I remember some times that *I* was terrified" I continued. "When Scotty would throw you so high in the air, I worried he would *never* be able to catch you.

"Oh. Remember the time David was bringing you home, driving faster than he should and went to pass a car? It swerved out and he swerved to miss it, and our car flew into a barrow pit nearly tipping over? David was shaking, scared to death, and you started the giggles, thinking it the grandest ride ever."

Jonathan scoots off the quilt onto the grass, the sun burnishing his hair. "Oh, look how auburn your hair looks. Where do you get that from?" I ask. "I know. Your Grandpa Elmer had a red beard . . . er, a red five o'clock shadow, Daddy told me once. Grandpa Elmer died when Daddy was just about your age, Jon. Did you know that? And did you know Grandma Eva married another man named Elmer, after your Grandpa died? Imagine, two husbands named *Elmer*.

"Come closer. Come lie down," I coax, patting the ground. "I'll sing you a song." I sing several. Jon stays sitting up. "Remember Grandpa Ami? How much you loved him to sing? How much you loved fingering his mustache? And remember when you were little, how you'd pull Grandma's hair? You'd always grab hers and no one else's.

"How much *do* you remember, Jon? Do you remember Millie dog? When you lived at home? Do you remember the cabin? I know you've never forgotten your brothers and sister, even when they're away and can't visit. Scott. Mark. Kris. Dave. They all love you."

I sit up, then crawl off the quilt onto the grass. Next to my son now, I wrap my arms around him and kiss his neck. Jonny lunges sideways and we topple over, Jonny sprawled across me. We laugh. "You're a regular King Kong," I say. "You've pulled Daddy straight to the ground many a time, haven't you. I can't believe how strong you are."

I stretch out on the grass. It prickles my arms. I shade my eyes from the sun. This time I begin to laugh. Jon looks at me, curious. "I'm thinking about when I drove my new little Honda down to visit. We went for a ride to see the cows, and you reached up and yanked off my rearview mirror. *Clean off the car*. How did you do that?

"We went to the old amphitheater, where all of us used to go, remember? We sat under the trees. Afterwards, I couldn't get you back into the car. You wouldn't budge. I wasn't strong enough to lift you. Oh, Jon. You're some kind of boy, aren't you?" We are quiet for a while. Jon bends over, resting his head on my stomach. I run my

Joy and Pain

fingers through his hair. "Mama loves you, Jonny. Always remember that, okay?"

∞∞∞

Several days after our visit to Jon, Dick rushed in from shopping with just enough time to unload the grocery bags before taking off. Today I was able to put things away. I never knew from day to day what I might manage. Into the crisper went lettuce, tomatoes, and a cucumber—with spoiled spots eating through its waxy coat.

The alfalfa sprouts were nicely green on top but the roots yellowed and gooey. I tossed the carton aside. Grapes, bread, oranges. Cauliflower? That wasn't on the list. No broccoli? Ignoring bruises on the apples and the tightening in my stomach, I continued unloading. Despite periodic shopping tips I kindly proffered Dick, I shouldn't carry unrealistic expectations. After all, he *hates* shopping, his natural shopping aptitude as woefully lacking as my natural aptitude for mathematics.

A few minor mix-ups and poor choices—again—were of no consequence. My heart welled with gladness that Dick even shopped in the first place. Such a sweetheart. And he tried so hard.

Aspartame? He got the brand with *Aspartame*—after explicit instructions to the contrary?

One last item in the sack. An avocado. It was soft. Very soft. Dark brown inside. This I knew without even bothering to slice it open. I breathed in slowly. *I'm in control. Totally in control. Acting, not reacting. Why, an innocuous little avocado can't possibly undo me. I'm grateful just to be up and useful. Grateful to have food to put away—with so many going hungry. Grateful Dick makes such an effort . . .*

"Ahhhhhhhrughhhh," I screamed, raising my hand then hurling the avocado to the floor. *Kersmuck.* There it lay, quivering, green-brown oozing from under its belly, like some mortally wounded mutant primeval protozoa. Congratulations. The morning was off to an auspicious beginning.

∞∞∞

It's not about overripe avocados, of course, or bruised apples. I know that. I've never thrown anything in anger my whole life. But I feel . . . so powerless. I'm so sick of lying here day after day after day. Yes. I know. *Sick. Tired.* Not the best choice of words to etch into my brain.

But I'm tired of being brave, of being cheerful and optimistic. Of looking for the good. I'm tired of life passing me by. How many more times will I stand at the door more likely lie in bed—smiling, waving good-bye and saying, "Have a great time."

I couldn't make Kris' Dance Club concerts and recitals. The boys' activities. Family vacations. Graduations. Seeing kids off at the airport. I've missed the chance to hold grandbabies, just minutes or

Joy and Pain

hours old.

I want to pick out my own lipstick and scrub a floor. Weed the garden. Jump in the car and visit Jon. I want to fly to Dakota and see Mom. Go to lunch with friends. Oh, I'm so tired of being a recluse. I'm tired of never being able to make plans, not knowing from one hour to the next if I'll feel tolerably strong or weak as a new-born kitten.

Frustration builds and I smack the bed with my fist. I'm so sick of lying here. Tears come. I curl into a ball. Sobs shake me now. Oh, Richard. All the times I haven't been by your side—company trips, your retirement party, enjoying your tenure on the civic boards you've chaired. I'm so proud of you. I want to enjoy your recognition. Enjoy gala festivities and interesting people. But most of all I want to enjoy *us*. Our going to dinner, to a show, skiing. Slipping off on some adventurous, romantic trip. I remember your saying the same thing, about missing us.

Exhausted, I force my sobs aside. Terrific. I can't even manage a bloody good cry! I lie quietly and wipe my eyes. What's the deal? Am I a ridiculously slow learner, or what? I don't understand, God. Did I misunderstand? Was it my hope, my imagination, rather than divine confirmation that whispered I would be healed? What's the purpose of it all? Haven't I learned enough from my illness? Can't I move on?

I have to pull myself up by my boot-straps day after day. I work so hard to keep positive, to use discipline in what I do or don't do. *It's a miracle that I have not gone stark-raving-mad* being down for so long.

I roll over, listening to my breath. In—out. In—out. *What good is my life?* What am I accomplishing? Maybe I'm being some sort of example about enduring, but that's the extent of my 'service' and 'contribution.'

And what of my talents? They decay from neglect. I haven't been able to do a watercolor or oil painting in years. Maybe I'll never be able to do oils because of the fumes. No sculpturing, either. I don't have enough energy to plunk the piano, let alone sing. Perform.

I can't even do my writing now.[1] My brain, it gets taxed and burned out. I can't even read, well, hardly. That was my great joy—reading. Helped keep my sanity. Now I can't even enjoy that pleasure. Or watch TV.

Why can't anyone get to the bottom of this mental fatigue? Why can't my doctors figure it out? Lying around all day is one thing, but not being able to use my brain? Vegetating. Vegetating. I listen to my breath. In—out. In—out. I can't do this anymore. *I won't.*

Suddenly, I suck in a quick breath, startled by a stab of enlightenment. *Vegetating?* Oh, Jonathan, it is *you* who can claim such a thing. *I've only taken a glance at being restricted, at being held back.* I've known your life has been a gift—from the day you were born. You sacrificed all that you might become, all that you might learn, all that you might experience and achieve in this world to be our teacher. Through you, by our service to you, we've had the

Joy and Pain

opportunity to be refined with a greater measure of charity and understanding.

I'm vegetating? My heart wrenches open to greater appreciation that Jonny's suffering and afflictions have been for our benefit—the purity of his soul, his nobility, far outshining that of any of us whose hands he's grasped so tightly, to lead, to heal and to love.

Suddenly, another bolt of understanding comes, but not from within my mind. Rather, it is divinely whispered. I hold my heart still, listening. I recognize this sense of 'knowing.' It comes, and with it comes a confirmation, just as the Spirit unveiled knowledge of a promised healing those long years ago—for I'm reminded about *knowing*. It comes, revealing new knowledge: *Before mortality Jonathan consented to come to earth with limitations.*

My heart floods with profound gratitude. Piercing through my angry grumblings and self-pity, this precious understanding is allowed to come? In my heart of hearts, I'd always believed Jon had some voice in the circumstances of his birth.

I let my tears wash my cheeks—wash all the traces of resentment from my eyes. *Oh, Jonathan.* I see more clearly all you have endured; all you have sacrificed; all you have suffered. I see more clearly the precious gift of your life. Still, I know I catch only a glimpse. One eternal day I will see and understand perfectly.

∞∞∞∞

Joy and Pain

SEPTEMBER 20, 1988. When Mother first went to South Dakota she stayed with Jay, Marilyn and their children. After a challenging year for all, Mom's increasing dementia necessitated that she move to a care facility where constant supervision was available.

During Mom's first months there, she was able in a limited fashion, to participate in some activities: craft projects, taking rides, enjoying entertainment. Her meaningful participation continually diminished, however.

Jay steeled himself for visits to Mom at the care center. When it was time for him to leave, she'd cry and cling to him, begging that she come along. The scenario became unbearable. Marilyn compensated, visiting often, Jay only when conscience demanded, the ordeal too painful for his tender heart.

Eventually, Mother lost understanding of who her family was: son, daughter-in-law, grandchild—merely sensing each person was someone important to her. One thing Mom never forgot was the concept of *home*. Where home existed she did not know, that hauntingly familiar place of 'belonging' etched into bone and sinew.

Every year I thought I'd be well enough to fly back, and even though I assumed Mom wouldn't know me, I longed to see her, to hug her and give her a kiss.

All of us kids wished Mom could peacefully slip away. Secondhand, Vel, Fran, Gary and I also felt the anguish and sorrow of Mom's increasing insensibility, the lack of quality and dignity present in her life. We were anxious for Mom to shed the trappings of this

Joy and Pain

confused, dependent, hollow stranger for the genuine article—the mother we knew, resplendent in all her magnificence.

Even though I'd fervently wanted to continue caring for Mom, I was glad to have some distance from the heartache. It had been four years since Mom had been in South Dakota.

On a Friday in September, a nurse at the center called to inform Jay and Marilyn, who were in Salt Lake City on a sabbatical, that Mom had developed pneumonia and was very ill. The nurse didn't expect Mother to last through the weekend.

Gary flew to Salt Lake from California and together he and Jay caught a plane to South Dakota. As with Dad's passing nine years earlier, siblings sat vigil over death and I longed to be there. While I waited-out the days, my feelings polarized. I was glad Mom was breaking free yet feeling loss and sorrow at her doing so.

∞∞∞

Tonight, I lay awake through the hours, an unending montage playing through my mind. Mother might last more days, yet tonight feels like my *good-bye*.

Ever so clearly I see Mom and me walking down the gentle curving slope of Panorama Terrace. I'd gotten a new India rubber ball. I skipped ahead of Mom, bouncing the hard little ball at an angle, high into the sky—two, three skips to catch it. Mom and I were going shopping. We'd take the Hyperion bus, then the street car to downtown Los Angeles where Mom would unearth wonderful bargains on fabric. Mom sewed most of our clothes.

We walked the hairpin curve turning onto Scotland. Scotland was steep. I continued bouncing the ball, running between catches. "You'd better stop, Sondra. You'll lose it."

"No, I won't," I countered. After all, I was extremely agile. Besides, if I missed a catch I'd simply run after the ball. What could possibly go wrong? Mom held her peace, a potential learning experience more valuable than a conquering of wills. I missed. Chased. Chased faster and faster. Then watched, horrified, as the small ball, whizzing along the gutter, disappeared through a drainage grate. Mom was smarter than I'd bargained.

The montage continued, unmindful of time sequence: Mom seated at the dining room table painting a watercolor; reading to me in that cozy floral chair by the window; pulling me, dripping, from my bath and gently toweling me dry; playing Chinese Checkers on vacation at Lake Arrowhead, letting me think I'd legitimately won.

I stretch and try stilling my mind this interminable night. *I have to get to sleep.* The images keep coming. I see myself at Sabbath worship service, seated on the hard wooden pew between Mom and Dad. It is evening and my eyelids hang like weights, the chapel lights softly glowing high above. I hold Daddy's hand, the one with his permanently split thumbnail, and lean my head against Mom's shoulder, nurtured in the security of their love.

I force the memories aside and glance at the clock, doubtful I've

Joy and Pain

drifted off between them. It's nearly 5:00 am. I'm utterly exhausted. Still sleep won't come. I wipe my tears then let the images continue.

I hear your voice, Mother, patiently answering my one-hundred-and-third question within an hour. The remembrance brings a smile. In floats a more recent scene. I see you at the sewing machine, sewing long sleeved shirts for all your grandsons; a daunting enterprise. I weep at the tremendous effort you've made.

Oh, Mom . . . why didn't I do more things with you before I got sick, when I had the chance. Why didn't I get a sitter and take you to lunch or to a museum; or to a movie, or window shopping—anything. I thought I was so busy. How terribly I regret not taking the time, our not being together more often, just the two of us—before I got sick. I'm so sorry.

The hands on the clock have moved an hour. My thoughts continue. *How blessed, how abundantly and marvelously blessed I am to have you as my angel mother. How privileged I am to be your daughter.*

I ponder Mom's forthcoming reunion, a heavenly host of loved ones waiting to greet her. Daddy coming, surely, to take her home. Home at last. Mother, restored in full measure to her magnificence and glory.

Suddenly, a jab of horrific pain tears into my reverie. From some place deep inside comes a terrible grief. *Oh, Mama. Don't leave me, Mama. Don't go. Don't go.*

I am astonished at the intensity. *"Don't go, Mama. I don't want you to go,"* the words continue in my brain as visceral sobs work their way to my throat. I clap my hand across my mouth, stifling them.

Wave upon wave of grief mounts then washes over me. Mother is dying. This very moment. Somehow I simply know. I let myself cry unrestrained, thankful I've had these private moments to grieve and say good-bye. Several hours later, Marilyn called to tell us Mother had passed away at 5:30 in the morning.

Answers

17

MAY, 1989. We were gathered for Mother's Day around our long dining room table. Time seemed to decelerate into slow-motion as I looked from one to another, savoring each loved-one's face. We had seven grandchildren now. Our two oldest sat side-by-side giggling, another was perched on a stack of phone books, one knelt on his chair, two squirmed on lap and high chair respectively, and the youngest napped in the bedroom.

Kristen sat across from me, helping cut her little one's food. Marv was seated next, then Syd, who was turned aside to the high chair. My eyes moved on to Mark and David, visiting together.

Mom Eva sat at the head of the table, widowed a third time, Elmer having passed away shortly after my mother's death. Eva looked youthful for eighty-three. Even so, a share of her wrinkles had to be etched by grief. She remained full of mettle, nonetheless.

I'd fed Jonny earlier. He was secure in his tiny room, the double set of stretch gates across each door. This proved to be Jon's last

Answers

Mothers' Day at home. Sadly, he would spend no more holidays with us. (We visited the Developmental Center or had Jonny home days preceding or following special days. "It's too stressful and exhausting to manage Jon and everything *else*," Dick had said. "He doesn't know the difference, anyway." *I knew*, but Dick was right.) I continued to gaze around the table. Scott and Glory's faces were in profile next to me. Lastly, I looked at Dick. My eyes lingered on his face.

I was deeply moved by my visual journey. I brushed away tears, glad no one had noticed, then turned my attention to the ensuing conversation.

"I swear I saw our old burgundy truck the other day," Scott said.

"Really," several of us squealed.

"It's a miracle that old truck survived our family." Mark laughed. "Scott, I can just see you floor-boarding it, wearing your hideous lime-green and purple cap."

"Floor-boarding?" Eva repeated.

"Oh, Grandma. If you only knew." Mark said.

Kristen chimed in, "Scott used to race along the steep foothills. Came close to rolling it many a time."

"How did you know *that*?" Scott asked, surprised.

"Mark ratted on you," Kris answered, grinning.

"Well, now. Speaking of ratting," Scott said, looking to Marv. "Do you know the infamous Truck Stories about Kristen?"

Marv shook his head *no*. Scott, complete with gestures and sound effects, described his brilliant idea to teach 10 year old Kris how to

Answers

back up the truck—so small she couldn't see over the dashboard. Inside our Karren Street garage, Scott could more easily load some heavy sheeting by gliding the sheets onto the truck bed as Kristen slowly backed up. Nervous, she'd slammed down the gas pedal and popped the clutch. The truck flew back, nearly running Scott down.

David picked up the narrative for the second story. Weeks later at Liberty—driving the truck through an *eighteen*-foot pasture gate, wide enough for two-and-a-half trucks—Kristen proceeded to ram the side post. "The post on the driver's side, mind you," David clarified, "three inches away from Kris' nose."

I loved seeing my family enjoying each other. Their closeness was the finest Mother's Day gift I could receive. Later, the boys set up the old orange Hot Wheels track on our staircase. I'd come across it recently. I watched their antics, racing the familiar little Matchbox cars that had belonged to David, the ones he loved to line up on the stairs, Millie watching.

It was a coup having all of us together. Some of the children lived out of state, and we had to share time with other sets of in-laws. What a treasured day.

∞∞∞

Years earlier, after a number of profitable sessions with psychiatrist Dr. Frank Garner, the doctor moved from Utah. Fortuitously, his move coincided with the completion of my brief

Answers

work with him. Also, my travels to Dr. Alan Beardall in Portland, Oregon, ended.[13] Additional practitioners came on the scene, helping me gain greater understanding about my health issues.

One day Jonny's former teacher, Kathy Terry called. "Have you heard of the Epstein-Barr virus?" she asked. I hadn't. Soon, it became a familiar topic to me. In 1988, the Centers for Disease Control (CDC) validated the existence of an illness called Chronic Fatigue and Immune Dysfunction Syndrome—CFIDS, later shortened to CFS. Among other contributing factors, the Epstein-Barr virus was implicated.[14] I was ecstatic to *finally* attach a bona fide name to my illness.

I was referred to Dr. Lucida Bateman MD, who limited her practice to CFS and Fibromyalgia. Her main role lay in diagnosis and suggested treatment. Dr. Bateman diagnosed me as meeting the criteria for CFS. She felt I likely had a predisposed genetic weakness of my adrenal glands and concurred with my having recently started medication for my thyroid. She also agreed that my episodes of lead, mercury and carbon monoxide poisoning had weakened my immune system. The onset of my illness, she believed, was a bout with mononucleosis I'd experienced in college. (Mono is caused by the Epstein-Barr virus.)

Dr. Bateman believed I fit into the most severe CFS case-scenario. Perhaps this served as the distinction why others could push, rest, recover and go again—and I couldn't.

Later research showed viral implication was not always present

Answers

in the syndrome. Also, specific bacteria or toxins were not always indicated. It was believed multiple factors triggered CFS, such as infectious agents, immune dysfunction, endocrine imbalance, low blood pressure and chemical sensitivities. Laboratory tests were recommended to rule out the existence of other diseases.

Doctors say long-term CFS patients do not recover, the illness is only managed. No known cure exists, although a number of drugs lessen some of the extensive symptoms. [16]

Also, I learned the human body does not differentiate between types of stress, physical or emotional. Stress is cumulative. CFS patients were encouraged to pace themselves carefully and avoid unusual physical or emotional stress. I was the poster child for push-crash. One of the greatest challenges of CFS is finding a balance within daily activities.

I discovered information about our bodies' electromagnetic energy field. I was more sensitive to alternating hertz of positive/negative currents than the average person, adversely affected by energy fields surrounding me. For instance, the computer, TV, radio, cell phone, appliances, the clock on the night stand and the electrical house wiring that surrounded me like a cocoon. My body was not only bombarded from these types of energy fields but from 'technological clutter' in our stratosphere as well, i.e., satellite transmissions, etc. [1]

How was I to live in our modern world? How could I actually implement all of this data? It was as overwhelming as the information

Answers

I'd received years earlier—in the packet from Dr. Theron Randolph in Chicago, when I first learned about Environmental Illness. I took a deep breath.

∞∞∞

JULY 4, 1991. Dick pulled off the winding road. The air was noticeably cooler in Little Cottonwood Canyon as we stepped from the car. Down the steep embankment, hopping from one protruding boulder to another—sliding on crumbly patches of dirt—we worked our way to the river below. How wonderful to be active.

The rush of water filled our ears. The virgin air was pungent with pine, leaf and bark. The river, full from the last drops of melted snowpack, flared wide above us, the water dividing itself against a huge moss-covered granite slab. Tall fir trees poked the sky. Cottonwoods interlaced an awning against the overhead sun. Thick undergrowth of willow and scrub oak screened the mountain slopes. Through an opening a towering peak loomed close by, verdant green.

Beside a tiny eddy, we sat down on a flat rock which hugged the riverside—the rock mottled with yellow-orange lichen. Dick leaned against a piece of granite that served nicely as a back rest. Slipping off my shoes I dropped my feet into the icy water, shock waves clicking my teeth. I lay back against Dick's chest. He placed his cheek against mine then kissed me there. "Love you," I said.

With his arms about me, we sat in silence under the dark, cool canopy, the river's roar in our ears. What a lovely way to spend the

Answers

holiday morning. My thoughts drifted to July celebrations our family spent in The Valley years ago. I missed those days: our cabin, the horses—feisty Macaroni Pony, Cinnamon with little Nutmeg and dear old Topaz, patient and wise. I missed them all.

Several years earlier, as the children moved out of town and my health was on a down-swing, Dick and I made the painful decision to sell our land and beloved animals. I would have to be content with my memories. Inevitably, life teaches us about change.

Across the river, a squirrel scurried by, interrupting my reverie. I watched until it disappeared behind a boulder. "Wonder what the kids are doing today?" I said, their faces filling my mind: Scott and Glory, Mark and Syd, Kris and Marv. Dick and I were glad David was living at home while attending college. He was boating at Lake Powell for the weekend.

Yesterday, we made an early holiday visit to Jon. Unbelievably, Jon was twenty-one years old, still looking twelve. Together, we'd taken a short walk and sat under the shade of a gnarly old tree. For the first time in his life, Jonny was putting on weight, looking somewhat chubby.

As Dick took Jon back to his room through the building foyer, he pulled loose of Dick's hand, galloped to an ancient piano and tipped over the heavy piano bench. Jonny managed to also yank a wreath off the wall, ever so pleased with his mischief. True to form, our son.

Snuggled in each other's arms, Dick and I continued listening to the river pound against the rocks.

Answers

"It's just me and you, kid," Dick said, kissing my ear. "So where do you want to go to lunch?"

"Hmmmmm. We could drive on up to Snowbird. Think it will be too busy today?"

"Probably not," Dick answered. I pulled my near-frozen feet from the water, folded my legs Indian-style upon the rock and cuddled back into Dick's arms. He took a sidelong glance, catching the smile that had begun tugging at my lips.

"... *What?*" he asked.

"I was thinking . . . I have no clue why except maybe because of that kiss on the ear. I was thinking about the time just after we got engaged, when we drove down that little alley by Aunt Virginia's and—"

"And parked and began smooching?" Dick cut in, laughing.

"And some lady came out on her back porch," I giggled, "hollering and shaking her broom at us. I was so utterly mortified."

"Yeah. Well. Truth be known, you were so chaste I hadn't gotten many kisses out of you up 'til then."

"Oh, my. Where have the years flown, honey?" I asked with a sigh. Silent again, we sat a while longer, enjoying nature's enthralling beauty.

"Hungry?" Dick asked finally. Nodding, I put on my shoes, stretched, then jumped up. "Beat ya to the top," I cried.

1937 Ami- WWI; Velma (left) with friend--Afton, Wyoming
Vel Dean, Gary, Velma holding Sondra, Fran, Ami and Jay in back

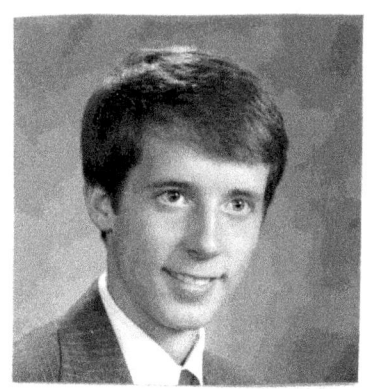

Scott *Mark*

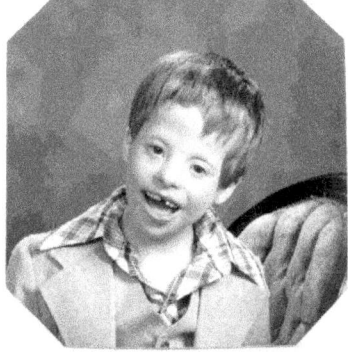

Jon, sporting his permanent lump and missing teeth.

1977

David *Kristen*

(back) Scott, Kami, David, Syd, Mark, Marv (front) Glory, Jonny, Sondra, Dick, Kristen

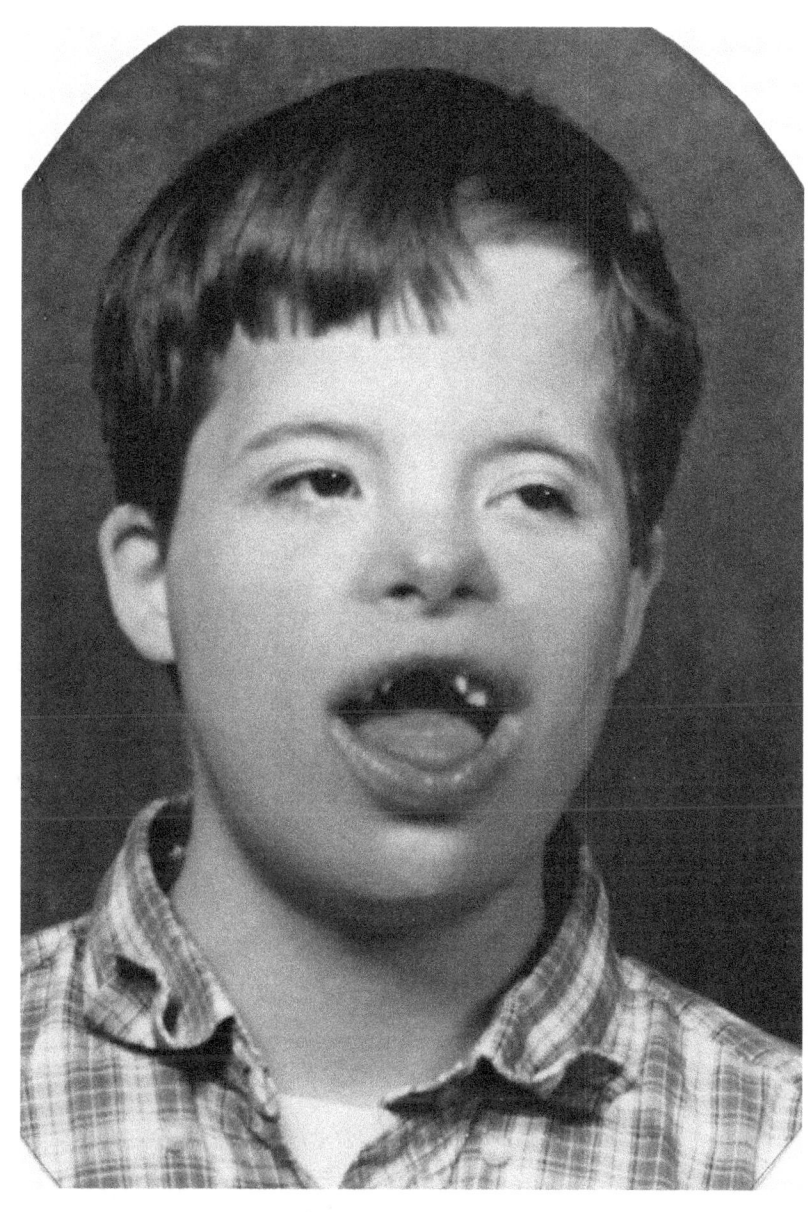

Jon, lookin' good

Grandma Velma, Sondra and Jon; Betty, Grandma Eva, Dick

Yo-Yos, Deck Chairs and Tulips

18

1993. Once again I was making consistent progress. With each period of improvement, I believed it to be the time of my complete recovery. Our days, sunlit with hope, were again pierced with dark discouragement as I came crashing down—weak and unable to function. "I can't handle this anymore," Dick said. "I feel like a yo-yo. Up. Down. Up. Down. This is insane going on for years and years. *I can't take being dashed to the ground again.*"

How perfectly he expressed my feeling. I could always jump off a cliff. Dragging myself up the precipice was the problem. Damn. I'd lost count how many times this had happened.

Just days ago, as I'd attempted scores and scores of times, I 'exercised,' walking slowly around my back yard, daily increasing a loop or two. That was it. Excited though, I thought this time I could finally sustain walking. I could finally build up my stamina.

Post Exertion Malaise Syndrome was the term used to describe the thorny condition. I thought, however, that I had been cautious and was using good sense in what I asked of my body. I thought with my knowledge of CFS I'd never again plummet to square one.

I asked myself: Why was it that other people with my condition, or a different debilitating illness, could push-through, rest, then quickly recover and I could not? I was not specifically referring to exercise. I meant, for example, being able to attend a symphony; take an art class; shop; visit a friend; take a trip. (Didn't I try hard enough? was I a wimp?) I knew the answer. Even so, the question lurked in the back of my mind.

What could I do differently? I knew of nothing. I took a deep breath and shrugged my shoulders, past feeling. Yet, deep down I believed *somehow*, Dick and I would *somehow* climb out the ink-black hole. *Somehow. Somehow . . .*

A sermon was coming on: I must take what life presents, seeking to understand what part I must play as life presents the same scenario time and time again. Did I get it or have I missed a lesson? Or do I simply need to master what I know in order to move on? Intent. Abundance. What I desire, what I envision, expect, claim, I receive. What I 'put out,' what I cast on the water faithfully returns in like measure. If I see my world as kind, benevolent and generous—supplying me with an abundance of good things—this will be my world. Not to say I won't experience challenge and trial. It's been long-established that through adversity comes opportunity for growth and ultimate joy. Mortal life offers a variety of learning experiences.

Marvelous lesson review. So, how does The Law of the Harvest apply to my illness? *To this miserable yo-yo scenario?* I'd always believed my illness could and would be overcome. I had looked for the good. I had expected it and received it. I had learned, grown and progressed. And, I didn't have to be absolutely perfect in learning my lessons.

Why, *sixteen* years later, was I figuratively sitting in the 'proverbial' deck-chair of an ocean liner—afghan draped across my legs, watching the ocean pass by while the other passengers played? What had I missed? Surely not belief, intent, that I learn and heal. *And not for a lack of trying. Enough was enough.* I sat in that 'proverbial' deck-chair sucking my thumb, enveloped in self-pity and darned sure I was justified to feel so.

It was one thing if negativity helped but it merely increased the blackness. At last I'd had enough. Stuck in the symbolic chair, I could look up—well fed and comfortable—and watch the passengers with lively interest. I could consider those whose lives had profoundly touched mine. I could enjoy the dazzling beauty of a sunset, glad to be on the trip. Voice Lessons.

I have no other valid option, really. I'll hang on, do my best, throw God's timetable into the equation and find beauty and delight in my journey. There are many types of healing besides physical healing. Surely I am becoming more whole—*aren't I?*

∞∞∞∞

Yo-Yos, Deck Chairs and Tulips

I developed minor kidney problems and picked up a viral infection in my pericardium, the heart sack. Complete bed-rest was prescribed. For weeks I had to stay put.

Throughout the years, my bed was covered with my phone, books, notebook and other items which lay scattered about. Inside an empty Baby Wipes box, my eye glasses, TV remote, lip balm, and pencil and pen were stacked, along with my eye mask and ear plugs. When I wasn't able to get to the kitchen, there was an assortment of Gerber baby food bottles, a banana, apple and a sack of almond nuts. A large bottle of drinking water sat within reach on my night stand.

I had fashioned a long hook out of a wire clothes hanger. With it I could drag something to me if it lay far away—if my energy level was too low to sit up or stretch over to grab it.

Who would or could believe such absolute weakness? There were times when Dick stood in front of my bedroom door, his hand on the knob, petrified to turn it and open up. He might find that I had died.

To my great distaste and mortification, I now had a bed pan within reach. A large glass Pyrex dish with its lid sat on a little stand next to my bed. Throughout the day, while Dick was gone, I was able to empty my urine into the dish for Dick to pour into the toilet when he got home. How humiliating to be so dependent. When my thoughts turned to others who were bedridden, perhaps suffering a stroke or paralyzed from an accident, my tears fell and I determined to keep my attitude positive.

Baby wipes came in handy for sponge baths. Once weekly,

Yo-Yos, Deck Chairs and Tulips

Kristen came to wash my hair. With my large speckled food canning pan on the floor to catch water, Kris sat on a chair straddling the pan. I lay angled atop the bed, my head jutting off the side while Kris supporting my head with one hand. With her other hand she managed to wet my hair with water from a pitcher, squeeze on shampoo, lather and rinse. What would I do without her? She and Marv had lived out of state for several years but had recently moved back.

Finally, when I was able to totter weak-kneed to the shower, I was overcome with the delicious feel of running water on my back. How much I'd taken for granted to be able to bathe and take care of basic needs.

I felt flooded by God's love. Back in bed, exhausted, tears leaked as I lay in wonderment. Because I was trying to focus on abundance and sincere gratitude, God was infusing me with comfort and hope—letting me feel His nearness. I could see a clearer image of the myriad blessings packed into my life. Whenever I manage to be appreciative, especially during trying times, I see God's loving hand. Joy outweighs pain.

Someone has said that God sends Love Messages to us. Gratitude clears our vision to recognize the messages. One morning, up from my bed for my allotted precious moments, I stepped to the window, filling my soul with the mountain's towering beauty.

A bird landed atop a bush, inches away. Never had I seen such a bird. It was exquisitely colored with iridescent blues and greens, its feathers shimmering in the sunlight. The enchanting little fellow stayed a long time, grooming himself and cocking his head as he looked about. With a peep, as if saying good-bye, he flew off.

Chance timing? Perhaps. I choose to believe it was a 'love-message': *I know it's tough. Hang on. I'm near. I love you.* I remembered similar feelings given me years ago as I sat on the tree swing, comforted at missing Scott and Glory's wedding in Arizona.

Not on an ocean liner deck-chair, but from my bedroom window I have watched many a spectacular sunset from beginning to end. When I steer my attitude toward gratitude I find and see many simple pleasures, reminding me of God's constant and bountiful blessings.

Days earlier, I was thinking how I constantly pulled myself up by my boot-straps; how patient and courageous I had been; how I'd not let myself go stir-crazy for being homebound. Suddenly, I recognized where my thoughts were taking me. *I was assuming far more credit than was my due.*

I did have to 'work hard' at keeping positive, at hanging-on and hanging-in, but recently I was not acknowledging my utter dependence on God and ignoring His constant outpouring of divine succor. I was ignoring the fact that He renewed me with hope time after time. By His tender mercies I was being sustained. I had not kept *myself* from going stir-crazy. Humbled, I offered a sincere prayer of apology for taking such grace and infinite love for granted.

∞∞∞∞

Yo-Yos, Deck Chairs and Tulips

There have been many angels in my life—family members, friends, neighbors, even strangers, bringing in meals, calling, sending notes, running errands, praying for me, coming for short visits when I'm strong enough. I have phone buddies, several with similar illnesses, who buoy me up on our reciprocal calls. We laugh, rejoice, cry, unload and commiserate, no judgments rendered. All these people who touch my life proffer sweet service out of the goodness of their hearts.

Do our acts of goodness to each other come from the wellspring of our own hearts? Doesn't God use us to employ His messages and His divine help?

When Dick and I were dating, one lovely summer evening we drove to a large park and pulled into a secluded alcove, shaded by an arc of trees. We sat in Dick's light-green 1956 Ford Fairlane, talking. I was leaning against the door facing Dick, enjoying his rendition of some college escapade.

Suddenly, I felt or heard in my mind, I know not which, an urgent command: *Lock your door, roll up your window and leave immediately.*

I whipped around, jammed down the lock with one hand and began winding the window knob with the other. I glanced to Dick ready to holler for him to do likewise. He was already rolling up his window. Dick started the engine and we pulled out onto the road, no words spoken.

The exact instruction had come to both of us. We had not seen a soul, but without doubt we would have been in grave danger had we remained. I do not know by what means the instruction came. I think, however, the impression did not come from within ourselves.

Ultimately, it doesn't matter how we received pure enlightenment—from our conscious mind, from our spirit-self within, or from divine power. All light and truth emanate from God—God being the author of truth and goodness.

I have a dear friend, Kim Day, who has suffered a long-term illness. Several years ago Kim stepped from her doctor's office into an overcast slate-grey morning. The air held just enough warmth to begin melting the last patches of crusted snow, but not enough to warm the bones or soul.

The news she'd received concerning her health had been disheartening. Home now, Kim crawled into bed, leaving her little son to entertain himself. For years she'd been unable to care for her children as she longed to, let alone have strength to nourish herself. Being a single mom and carrying financial burdens—*now to have additional health issues?*

Kim picked up the phone and dialed her mom, needing a talk. There was no answer. She tried a friend. No answer. Kim prayed, seeking comfort. It felt like no one was *home* there, either. Her exhaustion seemed to drain her prayers of sufficient power for lift-off. Someone needed to pray for her. Thumbing through her little directory Kim found a prayer-number she'd scribbled down one day. She dialed. Busy. Minutes later, still busy. Utterly drained, Kim could

Yo-Yos, Deck Chairs and Tulips

do nothing but weep. Never had she felt so soul-dark alone.

A few blocks away, a neighbor of Kim's was grocery shopping. As the woman pushed her cart past a flower display she heard a voice say, "Kim Day needs a tulip plant today." The voice was so distinct that the woman turned around to see who was speaking. The aisle was empty. The neighbor did not personally know Kim although she knew who Kim was. She picked up the pot of tulips and held it for a moment. Kim would think her crazy, showing up on her doorstep with flowers. What would she say? She put the pot back, ready to move on.

"Kim Day needs tulips today." the voice repeated again. Nervous and perplexed, she nonetheless grabbed the plant and put it in her cart. Later, still amazed and very nervous, the woman stood on Kim's doorstep, tulips in hand. Kim's little boy answered the doorbell saying his mama was sick. Handing him the flowers, which now held a card with her name, she fled.

Shortly afterwards, Kim called her neighbor and each shared their side of the story. Earlier in the week, Kim had been shopping at the same grocery. Passing the lovely tulip plants in full bloom, Kim had wished she could splurge and buy one. To Kim, tulips were a symbol of hope and of God's renewing love. She could certainly use some cheering and renewed hope about now. She sighed, pushing the cart on by. Oh, how she longed to have one of those tulips.

Yo-Yos, Deck Chairs and Tulips

At the conclusion of Kim's account, the women wept. Her newfound friend said, "Oh, Kim. I was just privileged to be the delivery person. God sent you those tulips."

19

NOVEMBER, 1993. Most of my hours were still spent in bed. What a boring scenario. What I needed was a good laugh. Comic relief was provided by a solicitation phone call from *Products of the Blind.*

"...Sorry, but I bought something from you guys a few weeks ago," I said. (I had.)

"Really? Well, will you help us out again today?"

"Gee, I'm sorry. (I was) I just recently bought something from Handicapped Workers. In fact, something from two different organizations. (This was true.) We're on tons of lists," I continued, "since we have a handicapped child ourselves."

"If you don't mind my asking, what did you get?"

What did I get? What an odd way to inquire about the nature of Jon's disability. "A Down's," I replied.

" . . . What?"

"A Down Syndrome."

Endings

"Ah . . . " the man paused, trying to figure out my answer. "I mean, what did you get from Handicapped Workers?"

"Oh. Garbage bags and light bulbs."

Weeks earlier, Dick and I found laughter amidst the frustrations. Dick not only had to run errands and do household chores, but now had to wait on me hand and foot, my having to stay put in bed for awhile longer.

We'd finally purchased a microwave, and one evening Dick fixed a vegi-burger. He'd guessed at the cooking time rather than checking directions. When I bit down, I nearly chipped my front teeth. I tried the opposite side of the burger. I tried sucking the patty to soften it then used my teeth like a file—not a particle came loose. I was hungry. One-half a bun, a tomato slice and a small piece of wilted lettuce just wasn't going to cut-it. I knew Dick was on the edge, so I was very reluctant to ask him to cook another.

Appetite won over reason. Thinking I was grossly exaggerating, Dick plucked the patty off the bun, intending to break off a sample. It didn't even bend.

The thought of all the 'cooking hassle' was just too much. *Everything was too much.* Dick pulled back his arm and flung the burger. Like a steel shot-put it whizzed across the bedroom . . . out the door . . . across the hallway . . . and, ker-thunk, it hit the wall— making a dent.

Endings

DREAM ON

*In my dreams
why aren't I a heroine,
street-smart, brave, true-blue;
triumphant star on my
own silver screen?*

*In my bedtime stories
I clean house,
forget lines opening night,
lose my class schedule
and stand on street corners
in my underwear.*

S.R.G

I'd dreamt all the misadventures, but my recurring dream was housecleaning. All night, it seemed, I was washing dirty dishes, stacking clean ones into cupboards; cleaning pantry cupboards, sorting, repackaging, throwing items away; cleaning bathrooms.

No difficult analogy here: mental/emotional cleaning, surely. Enough. I needed the mandatory fifteen minute work-break. I needed a *month's* worth. As I picked up a book of poetry, David came in, scooted me over and sat down to up-date me on his wedding plans.

Our last to marry, David had met Kamilyn through a mutual friend. He was taken by Kami's willowy grace and outgoing personality, her hazel eyes and long blonde hair, yet he didn't expect to get serious so quickly. Quickly as in courtship, not age, for David

Endings

was twenty seven now—just like his Dad had been when we married.

"We're so glad you stuck around," I said, "so Dad and I had the chance to enjoy you longer." Bravely, I was trying to keep tears at bay.

∞∞∞

NOVEMBER 11, 1993. David rushed in, so handsome, his face flushed with excitement and nervousness. "You look wonderful." I said.

"Well, this is it." I sat up as David knelt at the bedside. "I love you. I'll miss you, *Mommie*," he said. I treasured that special, endearing term he'd used when he was tiny. David said it only on special occasions now—a precious word engraved on my stack of 'recordings.' Voice Lessons.

In an earlier conversation I'd asked, "Do you remember much about me before I got sick?" I was worried he might not. [17] He did. I turned on the TV to pass the lonely hours, watching an old WWII movie.

∞∞∞

LAKE ARROWHEAD, CALIFORNIA—AUGUST 1945

I STOOD IN THE COLD WATER. THE LAKE BOTTOM WAS CLEARLY VISIBLE NEAR SHORE—THE RIPPLED SAND, THE LAKE WEED GENTLY

Endings

waving. Occasional clumps of willows grew at the water's edge, their roots fingering the fringe of moist sand. The tiny grains of sand gleamed in the sun.

Standing in the shadow of a willow, I searched for the polliwogs I'd come to see but found none. Several yards further I found a mass of them, shooting through the water like miniature torpedoes. Carefully, I dropped down and watched in delight.

A movement caught my eye. Through the trees I saw a man and woman sunning on the beach. My eyes did not return to the polliwogs. They flew wide open. The handsome young man was removing a pair of steel and leather prosthetics from his legs. I watched in nervous fascination. Pulling the contraptions free and tossing them aside, he leaned to his sweetheart and gave her a kiss. Rolling onto his side and positioning himself on his stomach, he pulled his body toward the water. The stumps of his legs dragged behind, trailing lines in the sand.

I averted my gaze. I was witnessing an intimate scene my eyes were not meant to see. I dared not move, afraid of being discovered—guilty.

In spite of myself, I looked again. The young man's upper torso was muscular and tanned, but it seemed to take great effort for him to reach the water for a swim. He had been a soldier, legs mangled in combat. My heart told me so.

Up to now, our country's heroes had been nameless and faceless to me. But there under the willows, the horrific price of war graphically revealed itself to my once-innocent eyes. Tears spilled. I clasped the palm of my hand across my mouth and sobbed.

AUGUST 14th, 1945

On this lazy afternoon at our Arrowhead cabin, I was stretched on the day-bed, reading. Mom sat by the window, sewing a button on one of the boys' shirts. My brother Fran burst in, interrupting the peaceful scene. "Something's going on," he shouted. "Come listen."

"Going on?" Mom asked, puzzled.

"Just come outside," Fran hollered as he disappeared through the door. Mom and I couldn't imagine what we might encounter. We obediently followed. "Listen," Fran cried.

I strained my ears. It sounded as if automobile horns were honking. If I weren't imagining, I heard occasional shouting. Could we possibly be hearing sounds coming all the way from the lakeside resort?

Horns honked nearer to us. Unmistakably, we heard

Endings

people hollering. We stood, perplexed. At last Mom cried, *"The war must be ended."* We rushed inside and turned on the radio. *Japan had surrendered. World War II was finally over.* Fran and I jumped up and down, screaming. Mom cried.

My siblings Jay, Vel then Gary appeared, and we shouted the news. Outside, leaping and twirling, we kids added our exultant screams to the other sounds of celebration. We would never meet those strangers sprinkled throughout the mountaintops above San Bernardino, yet we experienced a sudden kinship. We were fellow countrymen, bound together as we observed this momentous hour.

The next day, I sit at the rocky shore around the south point of The Cove. A dozen or so crabs crawl here and there, sideways, their eyes poking up like goo on a stick. What strange creatures they are. I sit very still, watching. My thoughts keep drifting away from the crabs. *The war is over.* The words drill at my brain.

I can hardly remember life before the war. What will it be like now? For one thing, when school starts in a few weeks, we won't be having air raid drills. Rationing will be over. Will we be able to buy all the chocolate candy and new shoes we want?

We won't have our school Victory Garden any more. All

Endings

The little military cards with the stars will be taken down. There were lots of cards in windows around our neighborhood. Blue stars showed a soldier was serving in the war from that home. Some windows had more than one blue star.

I don't like to think about the gold stars I'd seen. A gold one meant a soldier had been killed. I didn't like to think about a lot of things now. Like the pictures in the newspaper and on the movie newsreels, for instance.

Bombed-out cities, soldiers—thin as skeletons—who'd been prisoners of war. Refugees, eyes big and hollow. Lately, I've heard things, whispered things about concentration camps. I don't listen. I don't want to know.

I don't like to think about the amputee I saw on the beach, around the other side of The Cove. Much of my joy about the war being over is gone. I think about that afternoon by the willow trees. *I'm beginning to understand for too many.*

20

SUMMER, 1997. From the back yard of our new house in Sandy, I can see the roof line of our old home on Altavilla Drive, full of treasured memories. I'd found it as equally difficult to move from Altavilla as from our Karren Street home in Holladay. The care of a large home with three acres, barn and other amenities had become too burdensome for Dick.

One half-block west and south, our new house has the same view and friendly neighborhood, but not the overwhelming upkeep. Today I'm working out back, moving potted plants on the patio. In a while the girls will arrive from the Developmental Center with Jonathan—up for a visit. On such a nice day, we'll visit outside.

In a couple of years Jon will be thirty, no longer a boy but a grown man. His face is beginning to look more mature. His behavior is another matter, so I continue moving pots out of reach.

I think about all those who've watched over Jon through the years, at his home away from home. Beginning with Kathy Terry,

Universal Melodies

there was always someone who truly appreciates Jonathan's spunky, mischievous personality, his sense of humor, his basic good nature—even though he is more than a handful. Jonathan has been treated well by all, as far as I know. Always one special individual moves into his life as another departs from it. They come by divine design, I believe, surely not by chance. 18

After Self Help, Jonny lived in several different dorms. His family unit changed to all boys after he turned ten or so. Early on, Jon had been placed with a group of older boys. One particular boy began mercilessly harassing and teasing Jonny. I felt resentment toward the big bully, even though I didn't know the boy. Later, I was told a mother was irate at Jon because he bit her son. I learned to chill out, needless to say, understanding that the kids and parents both took their lumps.

For the most part, Jonny and his family unit of five boys got along fine. Jonathan has been with this particular family for years. He has his own bedroom and a closet full of clothes and favorite belongings. On the floor sits his large boom box (turned low). I'm assured Jon has his preference both in clothes and music. A Dapper-Dan with clothing, he enjoys Country Music and sing-along's. He doesn't like his stuff messed with.

Jonny does not have what could be termed a meaningful relationship with the other boys, but he feels comfortable and secure with them. Jon is, however, very affectionate with staff whom he particularly enjoys.

Universal Melodies

By law, Jonathan received an education until age twenty-two. Even though Jon's classroom was on DC property, classes were run by the public school system. Like every American boy, Jonny attended school Monday through Friday. I loved getting Jon's homework (scribbles), art work and Jon's hand print that were mailed to us on occasion. Focus was on Jon's behavior—learning to take his turn, attending to a task at hand, eating nicely and getting along with peers.

In 1992, Jonny and eleven other classmates his age had their Graduation Ceremony. Dressed in gowns, the students came from classes with varying levels of ability and function. After a heartwarming introduction of each child, a keynote address, speech and song by two students, the audience broke into wild applause. Graduation certificates were awarded. "We are here," the superintendent said, "to celebrate each child and teacher's caring, endurance, friendship and struggle. To celebrate day-to-day coping and courage; to celebrate every accomplishment, for with these special students, no accomplishment is small."

I was unable to attend, but Jon's teacher had the ceremony taped. Occasionally the camera panned to my son, yet throughout, I recognized Jon's noises in the background. Fidgeting, dearest Jonny amazingly managed to sit through that long exercise, behaving himself. I found myself bawling—deeply moved by the experience.

Upon graduation, residents are placed into Work Shop several hours a day, given jobs according to ability. They are paid for their labor. Jon's spending money is managed by staff, spent on treats, fast foods, etc., or saved for something important. Around campus Jonny has emptied trash containers, dusted, sorted and shredded papers, and made deliveries from one area to another—pushing items in a cart. Jon actually enjoys deliveries, I'm told.

A break from monotonous hours spent in the dorm, Jonny especially loves outings and the chance to go 'swimming' at the DC pool. He prefers the warm therapy pool, however. One morning, while making deliveries, Jon recognized the therapy pool entrance. Running ahead of the group and opening the door, he jumped in—coat, shoes and all—ever so thrilled.

On Sundays, Jon usually attends church. Still, because he's difficult to manage, Jon sometimes gets left behind during meetings and outings. "Jon has a girlfriend," I was told one day. For months, on rides in the van, Jon chose to sit by Mona. Mona even let Jon hold her hand. She was the only resident Jon ever paid attention to.

By the early 1990's, clients were being moved into the community, placed in group homes. The number of DC residents dropped dramatically during the following years, only the severely disabled remaining. Yearly, Jonathan has his PCP Evaluation (Person-Centered Plan). Parents, team-lead, direct care staff, social worker, speech therapist, nurse and psychologist meet to evaluate Jon's health, capacities, behavior and achievements. Short and long term goals are discussed. [19]

Jonny is able to feed himself, albeit wearing a thick, long rubber bib that sits atop the end of the table, dish attached. When Jonny throws things or tips over chairs, he cooperates when staff says, "Jon, pick it up, please." He doesn't throw or grab as often. That's progress.

For the most part—since Jon's stomach surgery years ago—Jonathan's health has been manageable, despite pneumonia, a broken ankle and a tonsillectomy to improve sleep apnea. However, Jonathan developed seizures several years ago. Thankfully, they have not worsened, but a big danger lies in his drop-seizures while he is playing or walking, causing him to fall.

I try not to think of Jon's broken jaw and the nightmare time of healing. (Jon often wears a soft helmet to protect his forehead, which sports a permanent lump, although it offers little overall protection.) Happily, Jon seems to feel quite well—still full of his normal exuberance. His health challenges are not visible, and I manage not to think of them often.

∞∞∞

"My gosh, you're full of it today, Jonny," Dick cries, rubbing his forearm which Jon has just squeezed—fingers like a vice. Jonny lets out his war-whoop and guttural noises, giggles, then lunges at Dick again. Knocked back a step, Dick manages to hold his footing and enfolds Jon in his arms. "Settle down, Jon," he says. "Give Daddy a big hug."

Jon wrenches free and like a defensive line-backer, rushes at me. I dodge as he drops beside me on his bed. He stays put an instant then scrambles up. I grab his arm, pulling him back. "Whoa, Jon. Stay by me," I coax, giving him a kiss.

Jon just reaches my chin, four-foot ten, but he can knock me flat. Dick, too. "Last time you were so mellow, Jon. Today you're like a tornado." Dick grins. "Well, Mama. We'd better leave while we're both in one piece."

Oh, Jonathan. You make me laugh. You're some kind of guy. Are you content, Jon? Or do you want to clear out of this old world? Physically and mentally you're headed on a downhill course.

I know your spirit-self doesn't exist status-quo—there has to be spiritual growth and development. So, what are you learning, Jonny?

Do angels visit you to comfort and help you? Are you able to hear when I send 'love messages' to you? What I know for sure, Jon, is that I'm privileged to be your mother. The day I was making soup while you sat in your infant carrier, I truly saw the magnificence of your spirit. I know who you are.

Oh, Jonny. It seems just minutes ago I first held you, first placed your cheek next to mine and sang you a lullaby. You'll always be my little boy no matter how old you get. But your spirit is eternal, mature and wise. If you die before me, will God grant us visits? Will you teach me things? Surely I'll feel your presence at times. I'll feel your love and encouragement.

One immortal day we'll talk and laugh. We have a whole lifetime to chronicle. What a joyful day it will be when you talk to me.

Universal Melodies

∞∞∞

MAY 3, 2000. Thirteen is Dick's and my lucky number. It takes the total of our grandchildren beyond an even dozen. Years earlier, with the eminent arrival of our first grandchild, I found out what all the 'pacing' was about.

No job is more demanding than parenthood. Nothing requires greater patience, courage, charity, humor, energy, endurance, commitment and wisdom! Like every family, ours struggles to find balance and cope with the demands and challenges of everyday living.

Humans interface with such differing backgrounds and ways of perceiving and doing things. Take couples, add children, then mix extended family together. What diversity. Relationships require all we have to give—and more.

Dick and I continue to face struggles. We are flawed and ever-so-human. Why is it I always need to be right? Why is it I can't leave that 'one thing' unsaid? *Try ten.* My old nemesis, perfectionism, sticks up its *perfect* head. Tack on my husband's hatred of being told what to do, let alone how. (Keep in mind Dick has to perform tasks no man was ever meant to perform: "Buy one-ply." "You put *Clorox* in my batch of silks?") Dick contributes a few foibles of his own.

We get past our rough spots by talking-out our feelings, by refocusing on tolerance, kindness and patience, by forgiving time and again and by looking for the good in each other. Positive or negative, what a person focuses on magnifies.

Voice lessons. Nothing is more basic than love. The greatest lesson I learn in life is to recognize and pay attention to the voice of love. Love facilitates recognition; love reveals the divine within; love reveals our uniqueness; love empowers me to forgive and extend mercy. Despite mistakes, love helps me to work in harmony with others. Love helps me to find peace in this wonderful yet troubled world.

Ultimately, my ability to feel and express pure love comes by opening my heart to God and receiving His divine grace to enlarge my soul.

∞∞∞

People write the script for their own life story, given the allotted general plot and cast of characters. Have I botched the job? Couldn't the lead character in my story-line leap off the couch, a veritable cyclone of energy? Couldn't she experience wondrous, thrilling adventures? Create monumental works of art? Do something grand?

I turn the years of my life over in my mind. My memories are rich with color; memories as varied as patterns in the old kindergarten kaleidoscope. Grief and pain, joy and success, disappointment and hope—each experience, each feeling forming and coloring the design. I've worked the pattern. I've written the story line.

Universal Melodies

I examine the script. I read aloud the dialogue of family, friends and associates. I read my lines. I hear our voices. I understand many lessons.

Both Jonathan's condition and my illness have taught me about listening, about waiting. There is a paragraph in my script describing God's promise that I be healed. *Why aren't I well?* I don't know. *Didn't I get it?* Some of it. Perhaps I'll still have full physical recovery. Perhaps the divine impression that came into my mind and heart spoke of a different kind of healing. I have sought to create a life filled with harmony and well-being. My efforts notwithstanding, God continues to speak peace and encouragement to my soul. He helps me find joy in my journey. He helps me feel whole. Yes, there are many kinds of healing.

I read a variety of scenes from my script. To my surprise, I find that many seem wonderful, exciting and fulfilling, replete with a grand cast of characters. I can't change the script I've already written. Surely, I'll botch some upcoming scenes, but I see with greater clarity as I continue to write. Perhaps that's enough, as long as I write with a loving hand.

There are three acts in the grand play. Act I—Pre-Mortal Life. Act II—Mortal Life. Act III—Eternal Life. In this earthly second act, with unnumbered scenes and players, I'm grateful to have my moment on stage—to have the chance to act my scenes. No stand-in waits in the wings to take my part. My life is not a dress rehearsal, [20] nor will I act in another performance; at least not in mortality. This is it. I remind myself the lines, the lyrics in my script are precious simply because I have the privilege to write the words and sing the melody.

※

JULY, 2002. I scribble my last entry in my College Ruled 3 Subject Notebook. It rests upon my knees, drawn up for support. I've filled the pages of a dozen or so. Out of my window, flowers cover the garden knoll at the end of the yard. The rugged mountains are backlit by the morning sun. I've come full circle.

I can't yet use our computer—the electrical field still bothers me. Besides, I last longer when I write lying prone. My energy reserves vary. Some days I'm up and about, managing light housework or pulling a few weeds from the garden. Sometimes I am able to go out to breakfast or lunch. I can usually attend family get-togethers and church on Sundays. Some days I can be even more ambitious, holding up for a short outing. Usually, however, by late afternoon I'm done for the day.

Interspersed among the good days there are times I'm basically down, exhausted, symptoms flaring. And so it goes. I look to the future with hope. In the meantime, there are songs to sing.

※

Universal Melodies

Dick walks into my bedroom. I push aside the stack of books, notebooks, papers and the old Baby Wipes box—still filled with pens, pencils, lip balm, my black satin eye mask, ear plugs, pocket calendar, eye glasses and the remote control. I push all my stuff further onto the half-side of the bed which still serves as desk and general catch-all for things I need at hand. The unsightly piles are mostly hidden by layers of puffy pillow shams.

I scoot over. "Come," I say. "Lie beside me." There's room for Dick now. Dick stretches out, settling his head comfortably onto the pillow. He pulls off his glasses and lays them aside.

I reach over and touch his cheek, then hair—white now. I gently trace my fingers across his face. Every little line and wrinkle I love. He still looks young, especially for seventy-two. I kiss his cheek then lay my head on his shoulder. I lie still beside the man dearer to me than any other on earth. Oh, Richard, you are my life's blood, my comfort, my strength. "I love you," I say.

I float back in memory to that June afternoon at Aunt Virginia's. "You might not remember me," the voice said, "but I met you at Don and Gretel's reception. Would you like to go to dinner and a show?" What if I'd kept saying *no*, or had simply hung up? I can't imagine life without this man beside me—this man who has carried his crucible through long, dark days and nights—and helped me carry mine. The crucible, the gift, shining bright with pain and love, teaching us, drawing us closer together.

I turn onto my side and snuggle in, draping my arm across my

Universal Melodies

husband's chest. His chest rises and falls with each breath. *Treasure every breath, Sondra,* I hear a voice whisper.

I drift back in memory to others I love so dearly; to Scott, cuddled in my arms as we rock; to Mark, face alight as he gives a good-night kiss; to Kristen, holding Lambie as she totters to me, laughing; to David, head soft on my shoulder as I sing a lullaby; to Jonathan, the spark of eternity unmasked in his eyes.

Dick's breath is steady and even now. He is asleep. I will lie still and quiet. I'll lie still until he climbs into wakefulness, until he stretches then smiles at me.

Again my memory drifts back in time to Mother, reading from the green leather book. "Little Gustava sits in the sun," she says. To Dad, whittling a whistle for me with the pocket knife that he always carries.

Listen to the songs in your heart, Sondra, the voice whispers. I listen to my song. I've been composing it since birth. I hear my melody intermingle with Dick's song. The children's notes come in, enriching the music.

My siblings Jay, Vel Dean, Fran and Gary's songs weave as a recurring theme through my life-song. Fuller and stronger the music plays as Mom Eva, Glory, Marv, Sydney and Kami's notes blend in. Still the music swells. I listen in awe.

I understand. Music flows in, generation from preceding generation. I hear my grandparents' songs, and those before them. My song is but a small melody-line within the grand, unending symphony. Yet my song will live on through my children, and theirs.

You sing your own rich, unique song—blended within your family score. Listen. Do you hear? One familiar theme plays within each of our symphonies, varied as they are.

I recognize the melody. I heard it that day when Jonny led me by the hand, as it were, under the great maple trees. The day my heart welled full, filled with the Spirit. The day I saw the magnificence of God's creations. The magnificence of you and me. Our magnificence—that is the universal melody.

Voice lessons. There are times I sing off key. I can't hit every note with perfect pitch and clarity. The important thing is, *I sing my song with love.*

CATCHING UP

How blessed I am to still have my precious husband by my side, 85 years old now. I'm following not far behind. We have 15 wonderful grandchildren and 8 great grandchildren so far, who add their unique melodies to our family score. Our children, and theirs, bring abundant joy and meaning to our lives.

Jon smiling sideways—his happy self

We find ourselves in 'reverse,' the ones who usually go to our kids' homes for holidays and have our children doing work we cannot quite manage on our own. We find it rather humbling and realize, now, that our parents faced the same scenario as they aged, with our being quite oblivious to their challenges.

Dick had a heart attack seven years ago, added two stints plus a titanium shoulder to his body parts, has neuropathy, gout, macular degeneration and enough variety of other ills to keep his life from

Catching Up

becoming a bore. We are lucky his health is actually quite good and are especially delighted to be together and have our lives so rich with blessings.

I am doing well, with good days and a few bad ones; a far cry from earlier years. My energy and reserves have improved greatly and I am able to stay fairly active during the day; evenings, not so much. Sleep issues are among my unremarkable health challenges, with enough variety for *me* to keep monotony at bay. I 'manage' my CFS. With Dick, I've been able to team teach a Sunday school class of teenagers for over five years. That is indeed amazing progress! They keep our faith alive in the goodness and talents of the youth of this grand yet difficult world.

*

Jonny still lives at the Development Center in American Fork, Utah. Throughout the long years of his residence, we have been tremendously blessed to have a number of exceptional care givers who have dedicated their lives in serving and loving.

Jon is 45. His health has badly deteriorated these last few years, yet his personality remains spunky and patient. When Dick and I visited him last week, Jonny was lying on his bed, resting. Nowadays, he does not lunge at us or pinch our arms. We miss that. He is barely ambulatory and spends a great deal of time in his wheelchair. Finally, he is looking nearly his age—*middle aged*. A few gray hairs are

Catching Up

appearing at his temples and his face looks mature. To others he obviously looks 'trashed' and noticeably 'handicapped.' To me, Jon will always be my 'little boy' and look wonderful.

On a recent visit, Dick slipped out to get a drink of water and I had a private conversation. My words were similar to ones I'd spoken years ago. "Jonny," I said, "I know your spirit-self hears and knows what I'm saying. Dad and Mom, well your siblings too, we are *so* sorry you don't feel good. We don't want you to suffer any longer." I gently touch the side of his face. "You clear out of this old world, Jonny, as soon as you can, okay?" (Several times, when Jon was seriously ill, Dick had blessed him to be released from mortality, 'giving' him to the Lord.)

"Don't stay because of us … we will miss you so very, very much, but we want you to move on—to be *free,* to be your true self, bright and talented . . . and unencumbered." I wipe away tears running from my eyes. "All of us, everybody, we can learn and grow without you . . . you don't need to be our 'teacher' any longer, to sacrifice being who you *really* are." Jon lifts his eyes to me for a moment.

"Oh, Jonny. I'm so blessed and honored to be your Mom." My thoughts flash back to the moment when he was three months old, when I saw his brilliant intelligence flame through—perceiving his eternal spirit: wise, beautiful and immortal. "You know how much I've wanted to have you home. To take care of you. To have you near. *Oh, how I love you, Jonathan J."*

Voice Lessons. I remind myself to listen more carefully. To remember what I've already come to know yet neglect to practice. To

Catching Up

play the songs I've recorded that are uplifting and beautiful. To chuck-out those which carry impatient, critical and ungrateful lyrics. I remind myself to have ears to hear and to treasure the universal melody, yours and mine, and to rejoice in its beauty and enduring magnificence.

*

Family remains our greatest bounty. Scott and Glory have four living children and five grandchildren, with one son waiting to greet us upon our arrival on the other side of the veil. They reside in Utah. Mark and Syd live in Oregon and have two children. Kristen and Marv, who have five children and three grandchildren, also live in Utah, along with David and Kami who live close by us with their three children.

Scott works with his sourcing firm but keeps busy as a volunteer fireman, Scouting Varsity advisor and enjoying activities in the Great Outdoors. *Glory* keeps busy with her growing family, a demanding church job and using her artistic gifts.

The clothing company *Mark* manages and designs for recently changed ownership, and he has difficulty finding time for his talents, myriad hobbies and outdoor activities. *Syd* stays involved with family, civic volunteer work and uses her talents teaching Art in the school district.

Kristen and *Marv* own and operate 12 small retail stores. They enjoy the out of doors in their Southern Utah home. They most enjoy visits

Catching Up

from their children and grandchildren. Kristen recently joined a local symphony, and Marv enjoys riding his bike year round.

David is a commercial airline pilot. He finds time to spend with his family and to enjoy cycling, skiing and camping. *Kami* is the favorite in her Pre-School teaching job yet remains a full-time mom, finding it hard to believe their first child will be off to college.

Sondra. One of my favorite occurrences is when I happen to dream about Jon—*he talks to me.* I also love it when Millie shows up in a dream along with my kids when they were little. Two homes have occurred in my dreams: Panorama Terrace and Karen Street . . . how I love those dreams.

Catching Up

EXTENDED FAMILY

Betty Dumm, Dick's sister, passed away February 9, 1998. He said of his sister, "Betty was one of a kind, outgoing and talkative. One day the phone rang at Betty's home. Her husband, Paul, heard her chatting for twenty minutes or so. "Who was that?" he asked. "Don't know. Wrong number," Betty answered.

Eva Yates, Dick's mother, was active physically and mentally until the last several years of her life. Yard and housework finally became too much and Eva moved to a retirement center, enjoying activities and friendships. As memory faded and interaction with family/friends diminished, she remained kind and optimistic.

After Betty's passing, Dick filled the void, visiting his mother twice weekly. He was incredibly sweet and attentive, clipping her toenails, rubbing lotion on her feet, taking her to the doctor and managing finances, for example. At the end, his mother recognized none but her beloved son. Eva passed away September 20, 2001 at age 95.

*

In high school *Dad* participated in the drama club. He gave readings on occasion and even wrote some poetry. I've mentioned *Mom* not only wrote plays but directed them as well. She was the acting coach, set designer, prompter, sound technician and make-up artist—all tied into one. It is still amazing to me. Mom and dad's 'artistic genes' flowed

Catching Up

through us kids' veins. So, how did our genetic/environmental creative inheritance play out?

When Jay was 4, Mom enrolled him at the Hal Roach Movie Studio, Baby Star Division. Jay was accepted to play in a movie called *Give Me My Quarterback*. The little actors wore football helmets, shoulder pads, and a diaper with a huge safety pin in the front. One of Jay's co-stars happened to be named Shirley Temple. (Vel was supposed to be a cheerleader in the film, but ended up bawling and lost her chance.)

We kids, at one time or another, had roles in Mom's plays. In 1946, when I was nine, Gary and I were in one of Mom's plays, performed at our church house. The general public was invited. In those days, talent scouts working for the movie industry frequented local productions. A scout caught one of our performances. He believed Gary and I were talented enough to 'break into the movies.' Gary, however, spent the following year in Arizona helping take care of our Grandma Richardson.

A role became available for the movie, *The Long Night,* starring Henry Fonda and Barbara Bel Geddes, directed by Anatole Litvak. Although the movie was already under production, the part of Fonda's young friend had not yet been cast. So I, along with twenty-five other girls, auditioned for the role. Mom and I took the streetcar and several busses to the studio. I thought the adventure wonderful and exciting—missing school a bonus. I made each cut until only 3 of us were left. On my final audition, passing through security, I was taken to a huge sound stage where a scene was being filmed. I was ushered into Litvak's trailer. He chatted with me a few moments to make me comfortable, then asked me to read from a script.

Weeks later the scout informed Mom the role had been given to a girl whom Litvak had previously directed. The talent scout wanted my folks to sign a contract, ". . . because I know I can get Sondra a role. She can become a real star." (Now, *that* was salesmanship.) Dad thought about it. To my dismay, he refused to sign. "An actor's life is not the kind of life for you." And so, my big movie career ended before it began….and Gary's didn't even have a *'start'* before his ended!

Jay also had roles in high school performances, and acted in Nathan and Ruth Hale's Glendale theater-in-the-round (which later became the Hale Theatre in Utah). He is a gifted writer.

Vel Dean kept up tradition and starred in both her senior class plays. She

Catching Up

performed in a singing group, sang with a renowned southern California choir, and played a beautiful piano until she suffered a stroke a few years ago. She wrote/produced numerous vignettes for differing church activities.

Fran was not only a great actor but dancer as well, performing with the American Repertory Theatre. Fran toured the US, Canada and Mexico with Disney on Parade. He performed in and choreographed many church productions. Francis passed away 18 May, 2014 after several years of dealing with the aftermath of a stroke.

Gary was a Toastmaster MC, and became active in city politics. He uses his artistic creativity as a builder, and has remodeled homes for several Hollywood luminaries. Gary is a master woodworker, designing exquisite one-of-a-kind pieces of furniture and hand-carved doors.

Catching Up

ACKNOWLEDGMENTS

Thumbing through pages of *Acknowledgments,* I thought these particular pages the least notable of a book. I've changed my mind. Truly, every book is a collaborative effort. As a teenager I was asked to give a reading. Finding nothing to my liking, Mom said, "Write one yourself." I'd watched Mother sew, paint watercolors, design floor plans, decorate our home with warmth and creativity—and write, among other things. Perhaps a few such genetic capacities trickled through my bloodstream. Her words were all I needed to hear. Dearest Mother, I still hear you whisper, *"You can do it."*

A friend, John Knab, said, "Sondra, you need to write up your experiences." Without Dianne Killpack, I doubt *Voice Lessons* would have come to fruition. I wrote my manuscript by hand. Dianne had to decipher my near-illegible handwriting while untangling deletions, inserts, and following arrows which led to more changes—all the while correcting grammar, spelling and punctuation. *(Rough draft* doesn't do the term justice.)

My other benefactress was my sister-in-law, Marilyn W. Richardson, herself a published author. Marilyn helped edit my manuscript and offered valuable suggestions without my feeling one bit guilty or beholden.

Valene Cook jumped in giving encouragement, along with Jane Sumner, Michelle Coleman, Sheila W. Wilson and Char Zarbinsky. As doubts flourished, Julie P. Karlindsay stepped in as

Catching Up

cheerleader.

Finally, I express heartfelt gratitude to my husband Dick—who accuses me of calling him 'Richard' when I'm peeved with him—yet whom I also call *Richard* when my feelings are exceptionally, and often, very tender towards him. Incredulous at my candor about our lives, my dear Richard blanched, resisted, then ultimately supported my need to 'call it the way it was,' as I perceived it.

Second printing: Many thanks to Maria Allan, Teri Benson, Deor Jorgensen, Corinne Allen and Sherry Taylor. Jason Williams and Dave Lindsay were of inestimable help with the formatting process. How indebted I am to them! I extend a special note of appreciation to Rachel Kjar for her excellent book cover design.

Catching Up

ADDENDUM—2002   Chronic Fatigue Syndrome (CFS)

Fatigue and insomnia remained unflagging companions and I continued having trouble sustaining mental demands such as reading, writing and watching TV. I was bemused at my nervous system symptoms: I needed peace and quiet. I felt like *The Bionic Woman* (a character from the late 1970's TV show), sound magnified in my ears. For instance, a door closing the other end of the house startled me as if slammed nearby.

Acting as a detective, I ultimately pieced together the symptoms affecting my electromagnetic energy field: I noticed, while playing my tape recorder next to me on the bed, that I experienced a strange feeling. I felt it again when using the copy machine and as I started to learn the computer. I'd feel strangely 'out of balance,' hyper, yet tremendously drained. One day I assembled a small water purifier that used magnets. I experienced the same sensation. Finally, using a new sonic toothbrush I'd purchased, I fell into a full-blown relapse. I finally realized I must be adversely reacting to strong electrical and magnetic currents. I hadn't known our bodies had an electromagnetic field!

Research data concludes people living close to high tension wires—utility poles carrying major power lines, power plants or substations—have a higher incidence of leukemia than the general populace. Energy fields are not always benign.

From Dr. Theron Randolph, MD in Illinois, I had learned the significance of food allergy upon health. The most common foods to cause reaction are milk, eggs, wheat, peanuts, soy, nuts, corn, fish and shellfish. Also, a link is suspected between excessive sugar intake, food allergies, food preservatives, food coloring and additives and children experiencing hyperactivity, mood swings and learning disabilities. A growing number of children display aggressive, hostile behavior. Attention Deficit Disorder [ADD] and other learning disabilities are on the increase. Offending foods and chemicals have been documented as triggering destructive behavior and diminished cognitive function in certain children.

When the Centers for Disease Control (CDC) validated the existence of Chronic Fatigue and Immune Dysfunction Syndrome (CFIDS commonly shortened to CFS), I seemed to hear a collective sigh of relief from all those suffering the same illusive malady. Someone once asked if I had agoraphobia, i.e., a fear of leaving home. Fortunately, no, but I 'feared' not ever having the *umph* to leave. With the CDC pulling together the myriad symptoms patients suffered and affixed a medical term, it was joy beyond expression.

Now I could finally and fully heal, I naively thought. Unfortunately,

Catching Up

there was and is no magic pill for CFS; no known cure.

While multiple factors trigger CFS (as mentioned: infectious agents, immune dysfunction, endocrine imbalance, low blood pressure, chemical sensitivities, etc.) there is no definitive test to confirm CFS. Laboratory tests serve only to rule out the existence of other diseases. A number of drugs do lessen some of the extensive symptoms.

> *Patients are encouraged to pace themselves carefully and avoid unusual physical or emotional stress. A regular, manageable daily routine helps avoid the 'push-crash' phenomenon characterized by overexertion during periods of better health, followed by a relapse [from] excess activity.*

I read a list of common symptoms: cognitive impairment (this must be the reason I couldn't sustain mental exertion), sore throats and tender, swollen lymph nodes in the arm pits (I often had them), heart palpations, night sweats, flushing, trembles, eye pain with deteriorating vision, Candida overgrowth and sleep disorder, for starters. How well I knew each one. What a comfort to know my long list was not bizarre after all. I also came across an interesting report: In some countries the medical term CFIDS was often linked with electromagnetic energy depletion.

There is help and hope for CFS, as in assessing stressors; changing attitude, perception and lifestyle; deep breathing, laughter, relaxation and mild exercise; specific nutrients required by the body and proper rest and diet, to name a few. The National Center for Infectious Disease and the CFIDS Association of America cite certain patients' improvement with non-pharmacologic therapies such as acupuncture, aquatic therapy, chiropractic, cranial-sacral, light exercise, massage, self-hypnosis, stretching, tai chi, therapeutic touch and yoga.

Before I developed CFS, a glucose tolerance test showed I had significant hypoglycemia (low blood sugar). Cortisol imbalance can cause immune dysfunction. Since I commonly experienced rampant viral and bacterial infections, the cortisol/immune system interaction offered an explanation. I considered my knowledge of environmental illness (the body's inability to detoxify and eliminate harmful chemicals). These issues were contributing their part in my illness.

Prolonged sleep deprivation impacts state of health. Cortisol imbalance is a factor in sleep disorders. Insomnia remains one of my thorny challenges, despite my use of relaxation techniques and natural sleeping

Catching Up

aids. Finally, I took Ambien, a sleeping pill, in order to have some 'quality' of life. I had no doubt cortisol imbalance, Adrenal Fatigue and my CFIDS were inextricably linked. Throwing in Environmental Illness rounded out the picture.

Doctors say long-term CFS patients do not recover, the illness is only managed. Still, I hold onto the belief that I can be well, although I'm not yet CFS's paradigm of recovery, needless to say. My greatest challenge lies in not dipping into energy reserves—not 'pushing myself.' By the time I realize I have overdone, it's too late. *The hardest work I do is trying to rest and do 'nothing.'*

When I find myself at 'square one,' I often feel like giving up—for an hour, a day or several days. Yet, I do have a choice. I can continue being upset and overwhelmed, knowing I do myself no favor, or I can redirect my attitude/perception.

Which will it be? I choose to begin anew, to reevaluate stress levels in my life. What physical, emotional and psychological factors helped bring me to the edge? I choose to remember lessons I've learned. Why? Because I'll simply get worse if I don't make a course correction. Besides, self-pity and despair become very unpleasant bedfellows.

Catching Up

CURRENT NOTES—2nd printing

If you are interested, internet/media has up-to-date information on Chronic Fatigue Syndrome and like-illnesses. There are numerous informative web sites/links as well those dealing with birth defects, etc. Also, recommended literature and book lists are easily found along with bios of well known physicians/practitioners, a far cry from the beginnings of this work. With some digging, hopefully you will find what might be relevant to you.

The following are a few examples:
Wikipedia: Chronic fatigue syndrome (CFS)
http://www.cdc.gov/ncbddd/birthdefects/data.html
CFS:http://www.mayoclinic.org/diseases-conditions/chronic-fatigue-syndrome/basics/definition/con-20022009
ME(Myalgic Encephalomyelitis)
http://www.thegracecharityforme.org/what.asp
http://solvecfs.org/mecfs-resources/patient-resources/
Dr. Lucinda Bateman MD: sleep disorders:https://www.youtube.com/watch?list=PLbO5abv0daLX-evYrHDcLILNSrFT6j0nJ&t=23&v=w4OEGOCw3Dg
Hypothyroidism (Hashimoto Disease)
http://www.mayoclinic.org/diseases-conditions/hashimotos-disease/basics/symptoms/con-20030293
https://experiencelife.com/article/repair-your-thyroid
https://en.wikipedia.org/wiki/George_GoodheartClinical Kinesiology information: http://clinicalkinesiology.myshopify.com (click- View Full article)

Sampling of older books which remain noteworthy:
The Power of the Mind to Heal, Joan Borysenko, PhD
Women's Bodies, Women's Wisdom, Dr. Christiane Northrup, MD
Adrenal Fatigue-the 21st Century Stress Syndrome, Dr. J. L. Wilson, ND, Dc, PhD
You Can Heal Your Life, Louise L. Hay
Cross Currents, Dr. Robert Becker, MD
Newer:
The Emotion Code, Dr. Bradley Nelson;
Messages from Water, Masaru-Emoto

Catching Up

ON FORGIVING

If you or I did not give or receive the gift of unconditional love, the steps we must take to repair our past provide poignant opportunity to learn the lessons of forgiveness. Forgiving self. Forgiving others.

Forgiving might be the hardest *soul-work* we are called on to do. Be it understood, forgiving another of wrongdoing has nothing to do with whether or not forgiveness is deserved. Nor does forgiveness in any way imply acceptance of wrongdoing, nor a diminishment of harm rendered. Rather, forgiving frees you and me from remaining a 'victim.' It gives us the power to *let go*, to heal and move on with our own lives.

But forgiveness is so much more, especially when God's grace is needed to enable us to forgive. Therein lies our transformation. Whether in forgiving ourselves or another, God may further the work we cannot complete alone, if we so choose. Becoming a willing, open vessel, God cleanses residues of guilt or hurt. We experience God's pure love. He heals our hearts and by divine power enables us to forgive on levels we thought not possible. The only path to wholeness, to a fullness of love and peace, leads us to and through the miracle of forgiveness.

Throughout generations, parents have typically done the best they were capable of doing within their set of circumstances, with the amount of knowledge and perception each possessed. Parents parent from the script created by the *voice lessons* of childhood. Your parents

Catching Up

did their best, didn't they?

We are seeking to do our best as we walk forward in our journey of enlightenment. (Still, is a fundamental component of 'doing one's best' ignored? Taking responsibility for one's actions involves the use of agency, yet there exists a tendency to equate bad choice with *experience*—excusing accountability. Regardless of its recent fall from grace, there remains and will always remain a moral right and wrong.)

Mental, emotional and spiritual housecleaning is time-consuming, hard work, no question. We are gratified not to be sole beneficiary of our individual effort and our resulting transformation but when we clean up our act, our children also experience healing. (Unresolved issues are passed on.)

If you were not raised with gentleness, encouragement and love, have you looked at it this way? *Yours is the privilege and opportunity of breaking your generational chain of dysfunction, large or small, whatever its form: indifference, neglect, excessive control, verbal or physical abuse, etc.*

There is not a more difficult yet redemptive work than healing issues of the past, for ourselves and for our families. In the lives of family members, here or beyond the veil of mortality, our healing, our forgiveness can assist each individual, here or there, in his or her ability to also heal and move on. Those who have completed mortal existence and now dwell in God's grace and love desire our wholeness—desire that their earthly mistakes no longer create problems for us, let alone wreak havoc. Yes, we can break the dysfunctional chain linking

Catching Up

progenitors and progeny. Ponder the scope of your own healing.

ON HEALING

There are many differing paths that lead to the healing of the body and mind. There has been such an outpouring of recent scientific knowledge and advances in medical technology. Available, are a variety of healing modalities leading to health.

Dr. Bernie Siegel, MD, used an innovative therapy for treating cancer in children. In his book *Love, Medicine and Miracles* he asked his young patients to draw a picture of how they 'felt' about receiving chemotherapy and radiation. If pictures showed sunshine or other positive scenes, Siegel believed his patient would do well on that kind of therapy. If pictures showed dark, grey clouds, for instance, he felt other options could be considered.

He had come to understand the most important 'ingredient' of healing: Unconditional love. It is the most powerful stimulant of the immune system, he believes. Love can heal. Miracles happen, Dr. Siegel says, with patients who possess the courage to love and who have the courage to work with their doctors, participating in their own recovery.

We all have options concerning our mode of treatment, our choice of physicians or practitioners and whether we choose traditional Western Medicine, Eastern, holistic modalities, or a combination.

Catching Up

Studies show the importance of the Mind-Body connection, so our preeminent choices must come from a belief we will do well with the choices we make. We have the world at our fingertips, from books to links on the internet, with access to pathways of information concerning any/every type of treatment. How fortunate we are to live in this day and age, with its many challenges, difficulties and abundant blessings.

We can heal mentally, emotionally, physically and spiritually. All of our life experiences, positive and negative, can work for our good.

REFLECTION

I vividly recall the first time I received help from a neighbor. I'd been down for months. Scott was away at college. The other children were busy with school and activities. Dick was trying to keep balls in the air. With the kids' help, meals were prepared and dishes washed.

A friend insisted on coming to do some light housework. She tackled my kitchen: caked-on spills covered the hot plates; the fridge revealed items sprouting/oozing stuff that made a lab petri dish seem innocuous; and *there were ants*. I was mortified.

It took years for me to laugh about her kindly visit. It is easier to render service than to receive service. Each of us is called on to face life's challenges. Elizabeth Kubler-Ross said, if we shield ourselves from life's windstorms, we wouldn't see the magnificence of their

Catching Up

carvings.

Be thankful for your windstorms, your life-lessons, for they clear your vision to reveal your strengths, gifts, capacities and your divine destiny. Open your heart to gratitude. Find joy in your journey and smile when you discover ants in your cupboard. God bless.

Catching Up

VANTAGE POINT

Before me now
the butterfly opened its wings,
catching the sunlight with a blaze of burnished gold.
A filigree pattern veined the wings,
its design etched in exquisite detail.

An inner voice spoke,
and I knew then
what had formed the intricate arabesque.
Profound and reverent joy filled my heart.

Success and victory alone
had not worked the design,
but failure also.
Not integrity and faith alone,
but shriveled dreams and tears,
error and doubt,
discouragement and fear,
suffering and sin—
caught and held, intertwined together;
no experience a waste
within the metamorphic journey.

Growth and transformation
had slowly and arduously emerged from the cocoon,
leaving behind, tattered, repentant fragments.

Yet gazing in awe at the golden handiwork,
sorrow for misspent opportunity and abandoned dreams
vanished from my soul.
From this vantage
I could see the unified pattern—
whole, complete,
sunlit now and bright with meaning.

SRG

Catching Up

ENDNOTES: 2002

Chapter 1

1. Heelan, Will A., *Alice, Where Art Thou Going?* 1906. P D

Chapter 3

2. *Hush Little Baby,* lyricist unknown. Thought to have been written in America. P D

Chapter 4

3. *Bill Grogan's Goat,* lyricist unknown. Public Domain (P D)

4. *Where Was Moses,* lyricist unknown. P D.

Chapter 6
5. Maxwell, Neal A. *All These Things Shall Give Thee Experience.* P. 46, Deseret Book Company, 1979. © Deseret Book Company. Used by Permission, October 21, 2015

6. Wordsworth, William. *Ode: Imitations of Immortality* from Recollections of Early Childhood. P D

Chapter 10

7. The clinic was a-buzz. Rumor had it actor Robert Redford was scheduled to meet with Dr. Randolph to tour the unit (because of his great interest in environmental issues). Redford was on location nearby, directing his first film, *Ordinary People,* starring Mary Tyler Moore and Donald Sutherland. We patients kept our eyes peeled, but to no avail. We never found out whether Redford actually made a visit.
8. Churchill, Winston. *Speech to Commons,* June 4, 1940. Speech periodically rebroadcast.

Catching Up

9. Wallace, Oliver. *Der Fuehrer's Face*, 1943. In a Walt Disney Studios motion picture. PD

Chapter 13

10. During the 1960's, Dr. George Goodheart, DC, of Detroit, MI, developed Applied Kinesiology. One of Goodheart's most brilliant protégés, Dr. Alan Beardall, made several discoveries that added additional tools to the developing field of AK.

    Throughout the years of my illness, a number of wonderful care givers attended me. Their expertise was invaluable. In addition to receiving physical improvement, I felt supported and infused with hope.

11. Patricia T. Holland, "Filling the Measure of Your Creation," BYU devotional, 17 January 1989, speeches.byu.edu. © permission BYU Publications & Graphics, August 26, 2015

Chapter 14

12. Mom's Star Valley days were exciting—being stranded in a blizzard; lost in the wilderness on horseback, for instance. "With the first snowstorm, the cars were put in the barn where they stayed all winter. Sleighs were more fun. We piled in with straw, quilts and excited friends to dance away the night in nearby towns. Everyone came to the dances. Sleeping children were stretched out on benches while the fiddlers played away the hours. Near midnight the food was spread out and we went home full, tired and happy. We did this at least two nights a week and I must say those cowboys were the best dancers in the world."

    On winter mornings, in the little one-room schoolhouse with its pot belly stove, Mom often peeled off her students' shoes, holding their feet in her hands—by that stove, a thaw-out before class.

    One of Mom's friends, a girl named Lillian Bounds, was teaching in Afton. Later, she moved to Los Angeles and wrote Mom she was dating

Catching Up

a fellow who, of all things, was drawing cartoon characters for a new motion picture process called *animation*. Lillian became Mrs. Walt Disney.

Chapter 17

13. In 1988, Dr. Alan Beardall was killed in a traffic accident on the Autobahn. He was vacationing in Germany after a lecture tour in England. What a great loss of a brilliant mind; Dr. George Goodheart, DC. https://en.wikipedia.org/wiki/George_Goodheart

14. CFS: www.cdc.gov/ncidod/diseases/cfs/**treat**.htm. (search CFS, Fibromyalgia)

15. (See Addendum)

16. Becker, Robert, MD, Cross Currents.

Chapter 19

17. I wanted David to remember his mom water and snow skiing; golfing; sinking a basketball in the hoop; throwing a football; acting in a play; building a snowman; rappelling the giant maple tree, hooked into Mark's harness—not lying flat. With the other children married/away, David had been such a help to me—to us, pitching in, being there with support and encouragement.
    Through the years all our family has stepped in, picked up slack, helped Dick and I keep our sanity. We've palpably felt of their kindness, understanding, love and prayers. What a tremendous blessing.

Chapter 20

18. I've been told each resident has someone among staff who particularly relates to him/her. My heart also rejoices in this wonderful equity.

Catching Up

It is difficult to express my husband's and my heartfelt gratitude and appreciation to the many extraordinary caregivers through the years who have loved Jon, have been his 'surrogate family' and his champion—deepest of thanks.

19. Examples from Jon's PCP Evaluation printout:
JON'S CAPACITIES AND TALENTS:

- Generally has a pleasant and happy disposition.
- Has a good sense of humor. Likes to tease (within limits).
- Can assist with dressing and undressing.
- Jon is very social.
- Responds to one-on-one social situations with individuals/staff he likes.
- Can follow simple one-step directions.
- Can make some of his needs and wants known.
- Responds to swimming/hydrotherapy.
- Appears to understand object permanence (will search for desired items).
- Is very affectionate/loving (at times).
- Is very energetic and full of energy.
- Is very alert and aware of his environment.
- Expresses some preference (likes and dislikes).
- Seems to understand somewhat the concept of cause and effect.

SIGNIFICANT ACHIEVEMENTS IN JON'S LIFE
DURING THE PAST ONE TO THREE YEARS:

- Has displayed progress in learning vocational skills (pick-up and delivery crews and janitorial).
  Attending to vocational tasks longer.
- Has progressed in toilet conditioning skills.
- Is more cooperative to walk with a group during outings or vocational deliveries.
- Is more patient at mealtimes.
- Has improved table manners.
- Is more cooperative in taking his medications.
- Is enjoying, and is attentive in music therapy sessions.
- His social skills have improved overall.

WHAT WORKS AND MAKES JON HAPPY AND COMFORTABLE:
- Enjoys visits from parents and family.
- Enjoys mealtimes/eating.
- Enjoys being active and busy—going on walks, van rides and community outings.
- Enjoys being with and interacting with his preferred staff members.

Catching Up

- Enjoys bathing, swimming and water play.
- Enjoys being in his room with his personal items/toys (at times).
- Enjoys and responds to one-on-one attention and interaction.
- Enjoys playing on playground equipment (swings, slides, etc.)
- Enjoys attention (positive and negative).
- Enjoys listening to and relaxes when soft music is played. Becomes very stimulated when faster or loud music is played.

WHAT DOESN'T WORK OR MAKES JON UNHAPPY:
- Hand-on-hand assistance.
- Being teased by peers.
- Peers using/playing with his personal items/toys.
- Bright sunlight (Jon has cataracts).
- Noise and confusion.
- Restricting Jon's movements.
- Being overly hungry.
- When he doesn't have his toys (due to breakage or loss).

GOALS:
- Implement behavior support plan.
- Continue toilet conditioning program.
- Have increased access to recreational facilities and community activities.

20. Questionably attributed to Pastor Lawrence T. Holman

www.ingramcontent.com/pod-product-compliance
Lightning Source LLC
LaVergne TN
LVHW051042080426
835508LV00019B/1665